Sleds, Sleighs & Snow

A CANADIAN CHRISTMAS CAROL

Sleds, Sleighs & Snow

A CANADIAN CHRISTMAS CAROL

Edited by

Anne Tempelman-Kluit

whitecap

For additional information, please contact
Whitecap Books, 351 Lynn Avenue,
North Vancouver, British Columbia,
Canada V7J 2C4.

www.whitecap.ca

EDITED BY Anne Tempelman-Kluit
PROOFREAD BY Nelles Hamilton
DESIGN BY Elisa Gutiérrez

Drawings in this book are by Andrew Costen.
Many of this book's illustrations come from *Picturesque
Canada, Vol. 1 and 2*, published in 1882 in Toronto by
Belden Bros., and are not individually identified as to source.
The sources of other illustrations are identified on
their respective pages. Antique Christmas cards and postcards
are from the author's private collection.

Printed and bound in Canada

LIBRARY AND ARCHIVES CANADA CATALOGUING IN PUBLICATION
Tempelman-Kluit, Anne, 1941–

    Sleds, sleighs and snow : a Canadian Christmas carol / Anne
Tempelman-Kluit.

Includes index.
ISBN 1-55285-704-2

    1. Christmas—Canada. I. Title.

GT4987.15.T45 2005   394.2663   C2005-903046-1

The publisher acknowledges the financial support of the
Government of Canada through the Book Publishing
Industry Development Program for our publishing activities.

For Madeleine and Her Mopa
May All Your Days Be Merry and Bright

Acknowledgements

If the devil is in the details, then this book should be full of devils. In fact, it's full of angels: archivists and librarians who searched, suggested, and encouraged. Individuals such as Jane Sproule, whose enthusiasm never flagged and who kept us entertained with numerous, quirky Christmas sites; Dr. David Beatty, who made a project of tracing an author; and David Goss, who knows Christmas in New Brunswick so well. Rare books were discovered by Michelle Sproule, Annemarie Tempelman-Kluit performed miracles of detection, and Nadaleen Tempelman-Kluit ransacked Eastern libraries with the help of her computer. Andrew Costen somehow found time to paint and draw, and friends across the country offered precious family photographs and recipes. And to many other friends who helped by just being there and by still being interested in Christmas, thank you. Finally, to my husband, Dirk, who never once said, "Bah! Humbug!"—I couldn't have done it without you. ❄

Contents

15 INTRODUCTION

19 THE FIRST CANADIAN
    CHRISTMAS CAROL
    BY FATHER JEAN DE BRÉBEUF

23 LOG CABIN CHRISTMAS
    BY ROBERT RENISON

26 NORTH POLAR ATHLETIC CLUB
    BY FRANK RASKY

29 UPON A MIDNIGHT CLEAR
    BY MARGARET LAURENCE

35 CONSTRUCTION CAMP CHRISTMAS
    BY EVA MACLEAN

39 REVEILLON
    BY A. MARGARET CAZA

43 LATULIPPE FAMILY TOURTIÈRES

44 UNFORTUNATE SANTA CLAUS
    FROM THE 'SAINT JOHN GLOBE'

45 CHRISTMAS
    BY EARL ST. C. MUIR

47 CAPTAIN CARTWRIGHT'S
    CHRISTMAS
    BY CAPT. GEORGE CARTWRIGHT

49 LOST MOOSE
    BY DR. MARY PERCY JACKSON

51 A RAILROAD CHRISTMAS
    BY JOSEPH PAYJACK JR.

53 ANNE AND MORE
    BY L.M. MONTGOMERY

57 CELEBRATIONS AT THE JARDIN
    DE L'ENFANCE
    BY MARCEL TRUDEL

61 HOW SANTA CLAUS CAME
    TO CAPE ST. ANTHONY
    BY WILFRED GRENFELL

69 CHRISTMAS AT THE
    SOUR DOUGH HOTEL
    BY ANDREW CRUICKSHANK

71 THE FREEPORT ANGEL
    BY RITA MOIR

75 CHRISTMAS PARADE
    BY MARSHA BOULTON

79 THE TRAPPER'S CHRISTMAS EVE
    BY ROBERT SERVICE

83 THE FRONT-ROOM
    BY NELLIE MCCLUNG

87   THE INDIANS' CHRISTMAS TREE
BY MALI QUELQUELTALKO

89   ALMANAC
BY LAMBERT DE BOILIEU

91   COYOTE CAROLS
BY DICK FAIRFAX

93   THE TEDDY BEAR COAT
BY HESTA MACDONALD

95   MOVING DAY
BY UNA PATIENCE CARLSON

97   THE CHRISTMAS CAKE
THAT NEVER WAS
BY EVELYN JOHNSON

99   'GRANNIE'S' CHRISTMAS DINNER
BY GEORGE C.F. PRINGLE

107   THE TOY SHOP
BY JACK PEACH

111   THE SLEIGH-BELLS
BY SUSANNA MOODIE

115   COLD COMFORT
BY GEORGE HEAD

117   THE ERRORS OF SANTA CLAUS
BY STEPHEN LEACOCK

123   NEXT YEAR COUNTRY
BY JUDY SCHULTZ

127   A BARRENS CHRISTMAS
BY EDWARD W. NUFFIELD

129   MAN'S BEST FRIEND
BY C.F. HANINGTON

131   THE FIRST CHRISTMAS TREE

133   A CHRISTMAS KISS
BY GWYNETH J. WHILSMITH

137   A TRUE BELIEVER
BY NELLIE MCCLUNG

139   CHRISTMAS ORANGE
BY DAVID WEALE

141   THE PROSPECTOR'S
CHRISTMAS GRACE
BY W. MILTON YORKE

143   OLD CHUM AND SCROOGE
BY MARY PEATE

149   A VICTORIAN CHRISTMAS
BY EMILY CARR

153   SPECIAL PARCEL
BY RITA JOE

155   DINING AND DANCING
BY ROBERT M. BALLANTYNE

159   CHRISTMAS DIET
BY CLYDE AND MYRLE CAMPBELL

161   LOST IN THE MOUNTAINS
ON CHRISTMAS DAY
BY DAVID WILLIAM HIGGINS

171   OUR RADIO CITY MUSIC HALL
BY MARJORIE PRATT

175   THE LUMBERMAN'S CHRISTMAS
BY E. PAULINE JOHNSON

179   THE LUMBER SHANTY
BY GEORGE S. THOMPSON

181   CARROT PUDDING
A DOW FAMILY RECIPE

183   A NOTABLE YEAR
BY DEREK PETHICK

185   DOLL'S DELIGHT
BY BESS BURROWS RIVETT

187   THE PARLOUR SECRET
BY SARAH FRASER

191   MERRY-GO-ROUND
BY ANGUS MACLEAN

195   OUR FIELD OF TREES
BY BETTY AND HARVEY KIRCHHOFER

197   THE CARRILLONS
OF THE PINE TREES
BY GREY OWL

201   WEDDING JOURNEY
BY LARRATT WILLIAM SMITH

203   CHRISTMAS IN THE KLONDIKE, 1898
BY REV. A.E. HETHERINGTON

209   RED AND WHITE
BY FRED EDGE

211   WINTER CLOUDS
BY JULIANA HORATIA EWING

214   KAMLOOPS CONVERSION
ANONYMOUS

217   THE DOLL
BY SYD CLAY

221   ROCKET RACER SLED
BY GUS BARRETT

223   THE BEST SEAT IN THE HOUSE
BY MORRIS GIBSON

227   DECEMBER 26TH, ST. STEPHEN'S DAY
BY CHARLOTTE SELINA BOMPAS

229 A LOVE STORY
BY GEORGE STEPHEN JONES

231 SHOP DAY AND SUGAR BEER
BY GEORGE SIMPSON MCTAVISH

238 CHRISTMAS CUTTER
BY GEORGE H. HAM

239 QUEEN MAB
BY LADY HUNTER

241 DRESS-UP CHRISTMAS
BY HARVEY BULLOCK-WEBSTER

245 WILY FOX
BY WILFRED GRENFELL

247 PAPER PLANES
BY MARY PEATE

251 CANDLES FOR CHRISTMAS

253 THE SURPRISE
BY ADA L. SUDSBURY

255 GREGORYS AND GROCERIES
BY LADY HUNTER

257 GOURMET CHRISTMAS
BY KATHLEEN SLOAN-MCINTOSH

260 ST. MARY'S HOSPITAL
CHRISTMAS BAZAAR
BY FRANCES BACKHOUSE

263 CHRISTMAS MUMMERS
BY SIR RICHARD BONNYCASTLE

265 DOGS' DINNER
BY TONY ONRAET

267 TROUT LAKE CHRISTMAS
BY HENRY BEER

271 THE STOVE
BY ADJUTOR RIVARD

273 WISHING HAPPINESS
BY HENRY VAN DYKE

275 SUGARED IGLOOS
BY IAN AND SALLY WILSON

279 A WONDROUS SNOWSHOE TRAIL
BY ROBERT RENISON

283 CHRISTMAS
BY ALBERT DURRANT WATSON

285 PERMISSIONS

291 SELECTED LIST OF SOURCES

Introduction

While researching three earlier Canadian Christmas anthologies, I began to truly appreciate the vastness of our country and the diverse celebrations that take place at Christmas. Despite the differences in the way we celebrate, and the diversity of climate, faith, comfort, and distance, the desire to commemorate this day in some special way with family and friends, warmth and hope has always been the wellspring of this occasion. Every Canadian is touched by Christmas and the short, dark, cold days of the winter solstice.

From sea to shining sea, across frozen tundra, icy lakes, snowy valleys, windswept prairies, silent forests, and rocky, storm-bound islands, Canadian Christmas stories abound. A hot buttered bun or a Hudson's Bay feast might have been Christmas fare for early hunters and fur traders, while Arctic explorers held rousing games on sea ice. Isolated, hard-working pioneers in snow-bound homesteads, thankful for lightened winter chores, turned their energies to simple gift-making and to sharing a Christmas feast for which, in poor years, a hoarded onion might be the savoured highlight. Victorians in Upper Canada celebrated Christmas with elegant balls and the joyful anticipation of parcels from "home." Children of the Depression era expected little. They eagerly awaited their one-room schoolhouse Christmas concerts because Santa or Saint Nicholas always made an appearance. Somehow there would almost always be something to create intriguing bulges in their Christmas stockings—an orange, possibly a few candies, or a secretly made toy.

Strangers, friends, and neighbours were equally welcome to share whatever there was, when what was eaten was less important than who it was eaten with. Inevitably, there were bittersweet wartime Christmases, with loved ones far from home and the ever-present dread of a telegram bearing bad news. Lovingly groomed horses and dogs and decorated bicycles, the showstoppers of a modern Ontario Christmas parade, underline the nostalgia that Christmas always evokes.

As these wide-ranging stories that I've chosen illustrate, Christmas in Canada is a unique and wonderful blend of traditions and customs from many countries, dusted with snow or sprinkled with rain, perfumed by firs and cedars, and enhanced with family and friends. Through stories of the year's most universal celebration, this book illustrates how Canadian life has changed over time. Immigrants from around the world arrived here, often homesick and lonely, but drawn by the hope of a new life in Canada, a land full of promise. Few had much, many had nothing but each other, and yet when Christmas arrived they made it memorable. Memorable enough that in books, journals, letters, newspapers, memoirs, recollections, and reflections, old and new Canadians have chronicled their adapted and adopted Christmas traditions and allowed us a glimpse of their lives, and for that we thank them. ❄

The First Canadian Christmas Carol

Jesous Ahatonhia–Jesus is Born   BY FATHER JEAN DE BRÉBEUF

HURONIA CIRCA 1642

Take courage, men, take heart today, for Jesus Christ is Come,
The devil's reign is now destroyed, his bonds are all undone.
And list no more to what he says, your souls prepare for
other ways,
Jesus indeed is born, Jesus is born, Jesous ahatonhia.

The Choirs of heaven sing above, so listen to Their prayer,
And do not thrust aside Their Word, the Message is so fair,
For God Himself is born a Child, the only Son of Mary Mild,
Jesus indeed is born, Jesus is born, Jesous ahatonhia.

Three Captains, then, from far off lands had talked the
matter o'er,
    And saw the Star, the so bright Star, that beckoned to this shore.
    They followed on where it might lead, the Love of God
their greatest need.
    Jesus indeed is born, Jesus is born, Jesous ahatonhia.

For Jesus put it in their hearts that they should come to Him,
    They knew the Star would lead them well, just once its
light grew dim.
    As one their minds to follow on, where that star led,
where the light shone,
    Jesus indeed is born, Jesus is born, Jesous ahatonhia . . . ✳

from *Brébeuf in Song and Verse*—originally written in the Huron language, translated by D. Hegarty, S.J.

Born in 1593 in France, Father Jean de Brébeuf arrived in Quebec in 1625 and became a Jesuit missionary to the Hurons on Georgian Bay, near what is now Midland, Ontario. Although in poor health for much of his life, he survived many dangers, but in 1649 he was captured and put to death by the Iroquois. Very few Huron escaped his fate, but those who did passed down the words of Brébeuf's Christmas carol. In 1930 he was canonized, and to Roman Catholics is the patron saint of Canada.

Silvery Lake Dirk Tempelman-Kluit photo

Log Cabin Christmas BY ROBERT RENISON

LAKE NIPIGON, ONTARIO 1881

C hristmas has special significance in the north. The short days and long nights with star-filled skies prepare one for the celestial message that Christmas brings to man. The first Christmas that I remember was when I was six years old. We were living in our log cabin on Lake Nipigon. The Indians lived in birchbark wigwams. By December the great trees stood like shrouded Commando troops around the clearing, and at night the stars hung in the sky like diamonds in the rosary of heaven.

There were no mails during the winter in those days and no white children within a hundred miles of us. Suddenly an air of mystery which was hard to endure developed in our log home. Father worked every night in the cellar by the light of a lantern, and Mother tucked mysterious things away in a large box which was kept locked. We were told that Jesus was coming; that he came every year in the winter-time, to people who were snowed under.

On Christmas morning we children rushed down stairs with our clothes in our arms from the upper room where the only heat was from the pipe that went up through our room from the kitchen stove. We dressed beside the red-hot stove in the common room downstairs. Our Christmas presents were home-made: woolen stockings, beaded moccasins, and new shoes for each of us. And there was brown sugar for our porridge, and condensed milk, which tasted like nectar. It was heaven. That night I could not sleep because I did not know how I could possibly wait twelve months until the next Christmas.

It seemed to me a stark naked miracle, and so it was. Jesus always comes as a surprise and always when He is most needed.

The Indians tell the story* thus:

> 'Twas in the moon of winter-time
> When all the birds had fled,
> That mighty Gitchi Manitou
> Sent angel choirs instead . . .
>
> Before their light the stars grew dim,
> And wond'ring hunters heard the hymn:
> Jesus your King is born!
> Jesus is born: "In excelsis gloria!"
>
> Within a lodge of broken bark
> The tender Babe was found,
> A ragged robe of rabbit skin
> Enwrapped His beauty' round.
>
> And as the hunter braves drew nigh,
> the Angels' song rang loud and high:
> Jesus, your King, is born!
> Jesus is born: "In excelsis gloria!"
>
> The earliest moon of winter-time
> is not so round and fair
> As was the ring of glory on
> The helpless Infant there.

And Chiefs from far before Him knelt
With gifts of fox and beaver pelt:
Jesus, your King, is born!
Jesus is born: "In excelsis gloria!"

O children of the forest free,
O sons of Manitou,
The Holy Child of earth and heav'n
is born today for you.

Come kneel before the radiant Boy,
Who brings you Beauty, peace, and joy:
Jesus, your King, is born:
Jesus is born: "In excelsis gloria!"

*As imagined by Canadian poet Jesse Edgar Middleton in his 1926 lyrics for the Huron Carol, set to the same French folk melody, Une jeune pucelle, chosen by Father Brébeuf for Jesous Ahatonhia.

from *One Day at a Time: The Autobiography of Robert John Renison*

Anglican minister Robert Renison began his illustrious career in 1898, when he canoed 750 miles down the Albany River to James Bay. At Moose Factory he lived with the Cree Indians for 14 years and learned their language. He later became Bishop of Moosonee.

North Polar Athletic Club BY FRANK RASKY

Courtesy of Nancy Moulton

*T*heir wintering at Cape Sheridan was not without its periods of Yankee nostalgia and high hilarity. Christmas was a nifty occasion, you bet, said Borup. Physical training instructor Donald MacMillan had the crew pickaxe a smooth seventy-five-yard track on the ice for the meeting of the North Polar Athletic Club.

At twenty-one below zero, Mac was certain it was the coldest track meet he had ever organized. The Eskimo women, even with babies tucked into their sealskin pouches, were first-class sprinters in the fifty-yard dash. The Eskimo men put on a good show of boxing, thumb-pulling and wrestling. In the rope tug-of-war, Matt Henson was effective but rather too light in weight; the two-hundred-pound Dr. Goodsell was a bull in strength; and everybody agreed that muscular Captain Bob could pull the side off a ship. Borup, of course, was a shoo-in winner of the white man's sprinting heat, and MacMillan put on a dazzling display of handsprings and somersaults.

Neckties were obligatory at dinner. The meal included roast muskox, plum pudding, iced chocolate sponge cake, brandy and champagne, and Christmas packages of nuts, candy, and chewing gum. Afterwards there were raffles and disc-throwing contests. Prizes most sought by the Eskimos reflected the incursion of civilization: the men preferred cigars, the women scented soap. The highlight of the festivities was a dance exhibition staged by the Floradora Sextette. A giggling chorus of six Eskimo beauties kicked up their furred legs in a cancan number while the pianola played ragtime tunes, as well as "Annie Rooney" and "McGinty" and "Home Sweet Home." ❄

from *Explorers of the North: The North Pole or Bust*

In 1909, Robert Peary claimed to have stood at the top of the world —the North Pole. However, neither Peary nor any of those who sailed with him on the Roosevelt kept verifiable records.

Upon a Midnight Clear   BY MARGARET LAURENCE

MANITOBA PRAIRIES 1935

C hristmas when I was a child was always a marvellous time. We used
to go to the carol service on Christmas Eve, and those hymns still
remain my favorites. *Hark the Herald Angel Sing, Once in Royal David's
City*, and the one I loved best, *It Came Upon a Midnight Clear*. It couldn't
have been even near midnight when we walked home after those services,
but it always seemed to me that I knew exactly what "midnight clear"
meant. I had no sense then that there could be any kind of winter other
than ours. It was a prairie town, and by Christmas the snow would be thick
and heavy, yet light and clean as well, something to be battled against and
respected when it fell in blinding blizzards, but also something which created an upsurge of the heart at times such as those, walking back home on
Christmas eve with the carols still echoing in your head. The evening
would be still, almost silent, and the air could be so dry and sharp you
could practically touch the coldness. The snow would be dark-shadowed
and then suddenly it would look like sprinkled rainbows around the
sparse streetlights. Sometimes there were northern lights. My memory,
probably faulty, assigns the northern lights to *all* those Christmas eves, but
they must have appeared at least on some, a blazing eerie splendour across
the sky, swift-moving, gigantic, like a message. It was easy then to believe
in the Word made manifest. Not so easy now. And yet I can't forget, ever,
that the child, who was myself then, experienced awe and recognized it.

We always had the ceremony of two Christmas trees. One was in the
late afternoon of Christmas Day, and was at the home of grandparents,
my mother's people, at the big brick house. There would be a whole

congregation of aunts and uncles and cousins there on that day, and we would *have the tree* (that is how we said it) before dinner. One of my aunts was head of the nursing division in Saskatchewan's public health department, and was a distinguished professional woman. I didn't know that about her then. What I knew was that each Christmas she came back home with an astounding assortment of rare and wonderful things from what I felt must be the centre of the great wide world, namely Regina. She used to bring us those packages of Swiss cheese, each tiny piece wrapped in silver paper, and decorations for the table (a Santa with reindeer and sleigh, pine-cone men painted iridescent white with red felt caps), and chocolate Santas in red and gold paper, and chocolate coins contained in heavy gold foil so that they looked like my idea of Spanish doubloons and pieces of eight, as in *Treasure Island*.

The dinner was enormous and exciting. We had *olives* to begin with. We rarely had olives at any other time, as they were expensive. My grandfather, of course, carved what was always known as The Bird, making the job into an impressive performance. He was never an eminently lovable man, but even he, with his stern ice-blue eyes, managed some degree of pleasantness at Christmas. The children at dinner were served last, which seems odd today. One of my memories is of myself at about six, sighing mightily as the plates were being passed to the adults and murmuring pathetically, "Couldn't I even have a crust?" My sense of drama was highly developed at a young age.

When the dishes were done—a mammoth task, washing all my grandmother's Limoges—we would make preparations to go home. I always had my own private foray into the kitchen then. I would go to the icebox (yes, icebox, with a block of ice delivered daily) and would tear off hunks of turkey, snatch a dozen or so olives, and wrap it all in wax paper. This was so I could have a small feast during the night, in case of sudden hunger, which invariably and improbably occurred each Christmas night.

The day of Christmas, however, began at home. The one I recall the best was the last Christmas we had with father, for he died the next year. We were then living in my father's family home, a red-brick oddity with a rose window, a big dining room, a dozen nearly hidden cupboards and hidey-holes, and my father's study with the fireplace, above which hung a sinister bronze scimitar brought from India by an ancestor. I was nine that year, and my brother was two. The traditions in our family were strong. The children rose when they wakened (usually about 6 a.m. or earlier) and had their Christmas stockings. In those days, our stockings contained a Japanese orange at the toe, some red-and-white peppermint canes, a bunch of unshelled peanuts, and one or two small presents—a kaleido-scope or a puzzle consisting of two or three interlocked pieces of metal which you had to try and prise apart, and never could.

As my memory tells it to me, my very young brother and myself had our Christmas stockings in our parents' bedroom, and Christmas had offi-cially begun. We were then sent back to bed until the decent hour of 7.30 or 8.00 a.m., at which time I could get dressed in my sweater and my plaid skirt with the straps over the shoulder, while my mother dressed my brother in his sweater and infant overalls. We then went down for break-fast. In our house, you always had breakfast before you had The Tree. This wasn't such a bad thing. Christmas breakfast was sausage rolls, which we never had for breakfast any other time. These had been made weeks before, and frozen in the unheated summer kitchen. We had frozen food years before it became commercially viable. I guess our only amazement about it when it came on the market was that they could do it in summer as well. After breakfast, we all went into the study, where we had to listen to the Empire Broadcast on the radio, a report from all those pink-colored areas on the world map, culminating in the King's speech. The voices seemed to go on forever. I don't recall how my brother was kept pacified—with candy, probably—but I recall myself fidgeting. This was the ritual—the Empire Broadcast *before* The Tree, a practice which now seems to me to have been slightly bizarre, and yet probably was not so. Our parents wanted to hear it, and in those days it wasn't going to be repeated in capsule form on the late night news. I guess it also taught us that you could wait for what you wanted—but that's a concept about which I've felt pretty ambiguous.

At last, at last, we could go into The Living Room for The Tree. The Living Room, I should say, was the only formal room in that house. We did not live in it; it was totally misnamed. It was For Best. It was the room in which my mother gave the afternoon teas which were then required of people like the wives of lawyers in towns like ours. The Living Room had a lot of stiff upholstered furniture, always just so. It was, as well, chilly. But it was the place for The Tree, and it seemed somehow the right place, something special.

And there it was, The Tree. *Oh.*

I could see now why we'd been so carefully kept out of the room until this moment. There, beside The Tree, were our presents. For my brother, a rocking horse, two horses cut out of wood and painted white with green flecks, joined by a seat between them. Our dad had made it, for he was a very good amateur carpenter. And for me—wow! A desk. A small desk, found in an attic, as I later learned, and painted by our dad, a bright blue with flower patterns, a desk which opened up and had your own private cubbyholes in it. My own desk. My first. That remains the nicest present that anyone ever gave me, the present from my parents when I was nine.

It was only many years later that I realized that the rocking horse and the desk had been our presents then because no one could afford to buy anything much in that Depression and drought year of 1935. And it wasn't until long afterwards, either, that I realized how lucky and relatively unscathed we'd been, and how many people in this country that year must have had virtually no Christmas at all. ❄

from *Heart of a Stranger*

One of Canada's best-loved authors, Margaret Laurence was born in Manitoba in 1926 and, after graduating from Winnipeg's United College, worked for the *Winnipeg Citizen* newspaper. She married and moved to England, then Africa, before returning to Canada with her family to live in Vancouver. After she and her husband separated, she moved back to England and later settled in Ontario. She has won numerous literary awards for her writing, which include essays and children's stories as well as such novels as *A Jest of God* and *The Diviners*, both of which won a Governor General's Award. She died in 1987.

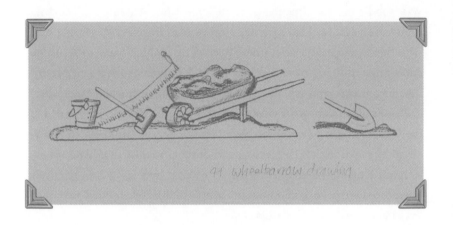

41 Wheelbarrow drawing

Construction Camp Christmas   BY EVA MACLEAN

HAZELTON, BRITISH COLUMBIA 1911

*W*e left about three in the afternoon of Christmas Day when they sent a team of horses and a sleigh for us. They would get us down to the camp in time for supper.

The snow was falling in large, soft flakes from a sky dark with clouds, not a breath of wind was stirring in the trees which lined the road that followed the winding course of the river.

We sat on a pile of straw in the back of the sleigh, well wrapped in blankets. The horse bells and our own voices were the only sounds to be heard. The horse's hooves and the runners of the sleigh were alike noiseless. Not a rustle broke the deep silence, the perfect quiet filled with peace on earth.

We arrived at camp just in time to enjoy a staggering meal. George, the cook, had certainly done himself proud with this Christmas dinner. Though he did not have turkey, there was prime roast beef, roast pork, roast potatoes and several varieties of vegetables and pickles. There was a Christmas pudding, mince pie, apple pie, cookies, and doughnuts. We ate so much we were forced to excuse ourselves by saying the long drive had made us very hungry. Immediately after the meal, we went over to the recreation hall and the crowds of men waiting for their entertainment. There must have been at least 350 of them, of almost every nationality. After serious talks by Bill and Dan, we settled down to enjoy ourselves in more informal fashion. Pails of candy and boxes of oranges were passed around, and I seated myself at the organ to sing and play for them. For nearly two hours I pumped that miserable excuse for an organ and sang song after song, the men joining in the chorus, until suddenly I was very, very tired. The men had been so appreciative and generous with their applause that I kept on long after I should have rested. But what was I to do when a Scottish voice called from the audience, "Bless ye, ye're a bonny wee lass, and d'ye ken 'Ye Banks and Braes?'"

It was that old missionary spirit again: I was all aglow with the feeling of having done something for someone, but I spoke up and asked, "Isn't there someone here who can relieve me for a while? Play, or sing, or tell a story?"

A middle-aged, shy-looking man named Lewis stood up and said, "That's the smallest organ I ever saw, but I'll try if you like."

I gladly but doubtfully relinquished my chair. As he seated himself, he turned to the audience and called, "Come away you, Williams, Davies and you, Rhys, and give me a bit of help, the little lady needs a rest."

I should have known that when there was a Lewis to play the organ there would be a Welsh quartet. Lewis, I discovered afterwards, held a high musical degree from the Royal Conservatory of Music in London, England, had been organist in a church in Wales, and afterwards in Winnipeg, before joining the staff of the railway company as a bookkeeper.

And now the Welsh quartet was singing with splendid vigour and harmony, after a few false starts. Before the evening ended we heard two fine Scottish voices singing the songs of their native land; an Italian who sang operatic arias as easily as we sang "Home on the Range," and although his voice was rusty from disuse, it was true and strong and he sang the loved "Vesti la Giubba" in true Italian style.

Last but not least, a couple of big, bearded Russians sang songs of the Cossacks with strong and resonant voices. To all the singers with the exception of the Russians, who were quite accustomed to singing unaccompanied, Mr. Lewis provided a spirited accompaniment, which must have surprised the bellows of that little organ.

By this time, I was a very meek girl. My vanity was whimpering and my social service was in full flight. I had thought I was bringing those poor benighted men something they hadn't heard in many a day. But now a suspicion was creeping into my mind, that it wasn't music that was scarce and precious. It was woman. Maybe it was because I was a young woman that made their applause almost an ovation at times, and that chivalry, or something else, made them so kind.

It was midnight before I was able to creep into my warm bed at Mrs. Marsden's tent. I fell asleep at once, waking to find her beside me with a breakfast tray with steaming coffee, ham and eggs, toast and marmalade.

By morning the weather had turned very cold and we started home immediately after lunch. This meal itself was a treat, as our hostess had roasted two ptarmigan which she had shot a few days before. They were quite delicious. She gave us three frozen birds to take home, and we were grateful for her skill with a .22 rifle. ❄

from *The Far Land*

In the days of the mining rush and the railroad-building boom in British Columbia, young Eva MacLean left her Ontario home to accompany her minister/veterinarian husband to northwestern British Columbia.

Reveillon BY A. MARGARET CAZA

I come from a small family—Mom and Dad, my brother, and me. There were Christmas stockings, a candlelight church service, gifts under the tree and Christmas dinner. And with that, the holiday season was over. New Year's, a week later, aside from a few wisps of "Auld Lang Syne," was nothing.

I expected no more, no less in my new station as the bride of a French Canadian man.

Six weeks after we were married, we celebrated Christmas by going to Midnight Mass in St. Anicet. It was charming. After Mass, we were engulfed in a blizzard of *Joyeux Noël* greetings outside the church, where Renaud introduced me to dozens of local people with names I'd never heard of. Names like: Castagnier, Faulbert, Dumouchel, Deschambault, Lefebve and Quenneville.

That was just the beginning. Renaud, who is the dearest, most sensitive person in the world in most respects, is infuriating in his belief in the school of thought that maintains a non-swimmer should be thrown bodily, and unprepared, into very deep water and will then, of necessity, learn to swim. Thus was I plunged into the local Holiday Season.

"Let's go to Ma's after Mass," Renaud said.

"All right," I agreed, clinging happily to his arm as we scurried through the milling crowd and drifting snow towards the car.

"We won't stay long," said Renaud, "but it's a tradition in French Canadian families for the children to gather at their parents' homes after Midnight Mass for coffee and a little lunch. It's called *Reveillon*.

Renaud's idea of a little drop-in midnight lunch turned out to be more along the lines my family might expect of a church picnic for an entire congregation.

After threading our way around the parked cars in the driveway, stamping snow off our boots in the woodshed leading to the back door, we went into the kitchen, where we were promptly mobbed by a tidal wave of the loudest, merriest bunch of people I'd ever seen, packed into the stove area near the kitchen door. It was a delightful, if somewhat overwhelming, sight, with welcoming arms hugging and everybody talking and laughing at once.

Savoury steam wafted up from the stove, with its pots of *ragout boulette* (meatball stew), chicken legs and spicy *tourtières* (pork pies). A long table in the centre of the room was crowded with baskets of crusty bread, bowls of salads, dishes of olives, pickles, and relishes. The buffet was aglow with candles flanking a chocolate yule log and mounds of cookies, squares, cakes, and macaroons.

I was suctioned along with the flow of the crowd that surged from kitchen to living room, and on the way caught glimpses of babies sleeping in the tumble of coats in the master bedroom off the kitchen. The whole house seethed with spicy smells and noise as everyone moved about, talked, laughed, and crowded into the big country living room where the Christmas tree stood waiting for the family gift-giving that would take place at New Year's. This worked well as a compromise for us, because it meant that Christmas could be spent with my parents, and New Year's with Renaud's family.

On that first Christmas, my French was nearly non-existent, and Renaud was the only one in his family who spoke English. Because he was

also the only one there I really knew (I sometimes wondered about that),
I clung to him with tenacity of fly to flypaper—though with his sink-or-
swim attitude he was far too busy being a totally involved member of the
family to translate the impossible volume of conversation that rose to a
raucous crescendo whenever the Clan Caza assembled.

from *Walk Alone Together*—a New Brunswick woman's humorous
account of the pleasures and pitfalls of moving to Quebec and
marrying into a large French-Canadian family

Courtesy of Claudette Latulippe

Latulippe Family Tourtières

My friend Claudette Sakamoto (née Latulippe) shared this very old family recipe.

TOURTIÈRE DOUGH

4–5 cups all-purpose flour	1 cup hot water
4 tsp baking powder	4 tsp vinegar or lemon juice
2 tsp salt	1 egg—well beaten
1 lb pure lard	

Combine flour, baking powder, and salt in a large mixing bowl. Measure 1 $^1/_3$ cups of lard and cut into the flour until it's mealy. Completely dissolve the remaining lard in the hot water. Add the lemon juice (or vinegar) and egg. Mix these liquids into the flour mixture until the dough leaves the sides of the bowl. Turn onto lightly floured board and knead about 1 minute or until all the flour is blended. Wrap in waxed paper and refrigerate 1 to 12 hours.

(If you use this recipe for a single-crust pie, make sure you weigh down the dough with dried beans or metal pellets to prevent it from rising when baking before filling.)

TOURTIÈRE FILLING

(There are many recipes for tourtière fillings. This is the Latulippe family one.)

3 lbs ground beef	1 large onion (my mom says "assez gros")
$^1/_2$ lb ground pork	Salt and pepper

Cook all the ingredients together. Add approximately half a teaspoon each cloves and cinnamon. (My mother, who didn't use measuring spoons, used half of a regular teaspoon.)

You can add a little water to keep the meat mixture moist.

Yield: two medium tourtières. ❋

Unfortunate Santa Claus

S anta Claus Takes Fire—A misfortune happening to Santa Claus is a misfortune indeed, and for him to become a victim of fire is an unheard-of thing. For many long years he had dropped down chimneys without so much as singeing his whiskers. This morning about eleven o'clock he came to grief while exhibiting himself in Mr. Geo. H. McKay's shop window on Charlotte Street. He was driving a goat that did service for a reindeer, when in some unexplained manner his whiskers of cotton wool ignited from a lamp which had been placed in the window to melt the frost. Instantly all was confusion as the whiskers blazed up. The reindeer-goat was speedily hustled out of harm's way, and Santa devoted himself to extinguishing the blaze, which threatened to consume his entire constitution. He tore off his snowy beard and stamped out the flames. The fire communicated to the scenery and draperies in the windows, and only the prompt exertions of Mr. McKay and his clerks prevented a serious fire. The store was full of customers at the time and a small-sized panic occurred. An alarm was sent in from box 27 but the services of the firemen were not needed, the fire being extinguished before they arrived. The damage will not amount to a great deal, and the loss is covered by insurance. ❄

from the *Saint John Globe* (now the *Saint John Telegraph-Journal*)

Christmas BY EARL ST. C. MUIR

PRAIRIES 1930

1925 Christmas Postcard

The frost is glistening on the snow,
The stars are bright, the moon is clear
The homestead lights are all aglow,
For Christmas time again is near.

In town and village shops are gay,
The festive spirit is abroad;
Tomorrow will be Christmas Day
In stately home and shack of sod.

In all these homes are tiny ears
That hear again the story through,
The story that for years and years
Has made the children's dreams come true.

In all these homes are little eyes
That sparkle bright on Christmas morn;
And Happiness and Joy arise
To greet that day when Christ was born.

The stars are bright, the moon is clear,
The bells are pealing far and wide;
The Christmas spirit of good cheer
Goes rolling onward like a tide.

Through all the land it surges on
Through storm and snow and bitter cold,
And every gift it breathes upon
It turns with love to purest gold.

from *Poems of the Prairies*

Captain Cartwright's Christmas

BY CAPTAIN GEORGE CARTWRIGHT

DOG HARBOUR (IN PLACENTIA BAY), NEWFOUNDLAND 1770

*M*onday, December 24, 1770. At sun-set the people ushered in Christmas, according to the Newfoundland custom. In the first place, they built up a prodigious large fire in their houses; all hands then assembled before the door, and one of them fired a gun, loaded with powder only; afterwards each of them drank a dram of rum, concluding the ceremony with three cheers. These formalities being performed with great solemnity, they retired to their house, got drunk as fast as they could, and spent the whole night in drinking, quarrelling, and fighting. It is but natural to suppose that the noise which they made (their house being but six feet from the head of my bed), together with the apprehension of seeing my house in flames, prevented me from once closing my eyes.

Tuesday, December 25, 1770. The people were all drunk, quarrelling, and fighting all day. It snowed early in the morning, the forenoon was dull, and the rest of the day clear, with hard frost.

Captain Cartwright fared better the following year:

Wednes., December 25, 1771. I treated all hands with buttered hot rolls and coffee for breakfast; after which, some of them walked up the river, where they saw the track of a wolf. I read prayers, and afterwards regaled the people with veal pie and rice pudding for dinner. In the evening I walked to Island Brook. The sky was clear, and the frost not so severe as yesterday. ❄

from *Captain Cartwright and His Labrador Journal*

George Cartwright, English soldier, entrepreneur and diarist, kept a journal detailing the sixteen years he spent in Labrador operating fisheries in cod, salmon, and seals. He also traded in furs. This entry is from his first year.

Lost Moose Dirk Tempelman-Kluit photo

Lost Moose BY DR. MARY PERCY JACKSON

BATTLE RIVER PRAIRIE, ALBERTA 1929

*W*hat a treat it was to get mail from home at Christmas time! It was simply of staggering proportion—literally so when I had to carry a big sackful, with drifts three or four feet deep across the trail. I got a Christmas pudding (the pudding basin was broken, but the pudding was intact, praise be). I also received a magnificent cake. The expression on sundry old bachelors' faces when they tasted it was a sight to behold. Cake like that they had never seen in Battle River Prairie!

There was no danger of my having Christmas all on my lonesome; I went out nearly every day that week and mortally offended lots of people by accepting other people's invitations first.

That first Christmas in Battle River an old bachelor trapper named Hal Reber offered to take me moose hunting. I got myself a big game licence, borrowed a .30-30 rifle, and practised shooting with it. Then I went out with him south and east of North Star. We rode single file through the bush. Hal ahead of me, looking for moose. Suddenly, quite close in front of him, he saw a moose. Quickly he was just getting off his horse to shoot it when one of the dead spruce branches of a windfall ran up between his waist coat and his shirt and he hung there while the horse moved away, as well as the moose. That was the nearest I ever came to shooting a moose. Obviously I couldn't shoot when Hal was in front of me, even if I had not been too dumbstruck, seeing him hanging there! ❄

from *The Homemade Brass Plate*

Fresh from urban England with stethoscope packed, adventurous Dr. Mary Percy was just 25 when she reached the Peace River wilds in response to an Alberta government ad for a doctor to practice in a roadless area where "riding a horse was an advantage." She stayed 45 years, marrying fur trader and farmer Frank Jackson.

Christmas 1928

A Railroad Christmas BY JOSEPH PAYJACK JR.

WINNIPEG, MANITOBA 1931

W e lived on Higgins Avenue of Winnipeg still known as Point
Douglas. Our house was about three blocks east of the CPR
depot and the now long-gone CPR Royal Alexander Hotel. Point Douglas
was a decent but far from affluent neighbourhood, at that time feeling the
effects of the Great Depression.

On Christmas Day, 1931, we were preparing to have our dinner. Our
family, also harshly affected by the times, somehow still was able to lay out
a truly festive table—turkey, root-cellar vegetables, preserves, and traditional Ukrainian fare. The house was full. Not only our immediate family
but uncles, aunts, and cousins were there to make it a true family affair.

There was a knock at the door, and my father answered. A young boy,
perhaps eighteen years old or so, stood before my dad and asked for a bite
to eat or a few cents. Without hesitation, my dad asked the boy in and
immediately made him feel comfortable and at ease. He had a way of making people feel welcome, and, so I have learned, was generous to a fault.

Dad proceeded to help the boy clean up, for he had just gotten off the
freight train. He had been "riding the rods" as it was termed—a common
occurrence in those days. The young man was given a clean shirt, and, a
short time later, our guest came downstairs to join our family for dinner.
He spent the night on the chesterfield and in the morning, after breakfast,
my dad rounded up some spare warm clothing, packed a lunch with
Christmas leftovers and, I was told, also gave him an undisclosed amount
of cash.

Three and half years later, on June 24, 1935, my father passed away from pleurisy. He was thirty-eight years old. This I remember well. He was well-known and well-liked, and needless to say it was a large funeral.

One day a few years later, my mother answered a knock at the door. The man facing her smiled and said hello. Mom thought he looked a bit familiar but couldn't place him. He asked if he could see Mr. Payjack. When Mother told him of my dad's passing, the man broke down and wept openly. Regaining his composure, he told my mother that the gesture of kindness displayed that Christmas in 1931 not only helped save his life, but it was a "stepping stone" to a new beginning. He offered my mother a sum of money, but she would not accept it, even though she probably could have used it. She just said, "That is the way my husband would want it to be." The young man left and we never heard from him again. ❄

from *Sunny Side Up: Fond Memories of Prairie Life in the 1930s*

Joseph Payjack's story is one of 30 from largely unscathed Great Depression survivors to be found alongside those of their compiler, author, and former rural Saskatchewan schoolteacher Eileen Comstock, who celebrates the resilience and spirit of Canada's Prairie folk.

Anne and More BY L.M. MONTGOMERY

CAVENDISH, PRINCE EDWARD ISLAND 1908

*T*hermometer 5 below zero. A raging snowstorm to boot. Frost on window panes. Wind wailing in chimney. A box of white Roman hyacinths sending out alien whiffs of old summers.

My dear Mr. Weber,

When I received your last letter on October 29th, I said to myself, "For once I'm going to be decent and I'll answer this letter next week." What is more, I really meant it. Yet here it is December 22nd. Well, I couldn't help it, and that is all there is to it. I've been so busy—and so tired. I'm still the latter. I'd love to go to bed and stay there for a whole month, doing nothing, seeing nothing and *thinking* nothing. I really don't feel at all well—and yet there is nothing the matter with me. I've simply "gone stale." If you've ever experienced the feeling I'm sure of your sympathy. If you haven't it's quite indescribable and I won't try to describe it. Instead I'll just pick up my notebooks, turn back to the entry of my last letter to you and discuss the jottings of any possibly interesting happenings since. I daresay the most of the letter will be about that detestable "Anne." There doesn't seem to be anything but her in my life just now and I'm so horribly tired of her, if it were not for just two things. One of these things is a letter I received last month from a poor little cripple in Ohio who wrote to thank me for writing "Anne" because she said it had taught her how to endure her long lonely days of imprisonment by just "imagining things." And the other is that "Anne" has gone through six editions and that must mean a decent cheque when pay day comes!

Well, it was September when I last wrote. We had the most exquisite autumn here this year. October was more beautiful than any June I ever remember. I couldn't help enjoying it, tired and rushed as I was. Every morning before sitting down to my typewriter I'd take a walk over the hill and feel almost like I should feel for a little while. November was also a decent month as Novembers go, but December has been very cold. Today as aforesaid has been a big storm. We are drifted up, have no mail, and were it not for my hyacinths I should feel inclined to stop being an optimist.

Well, I've done my duty by the weather, haven't I? Of course, one had to mention it. 'Twouldn't be lucky not to.

I hope *this* isn't going to last all winter—more storm and bitter frost. I *did* shovel snow as predicted—there's no one we can get to do this for us— it's all drifted back again. No mail still—and I'm ready to tear out my hair in handfuls!

Really, this has been a hard day. I haven't felt very well and am *tireder* than ever tonight. But I shall try to finish this letter—nay, I *will* finish it, even if I just have to *stop short*.

Yes, I want to see you settle down to some congenial work as soon as possible. Shake off as many of your metaphorical fleas as possible, resolve to *grin and bear* the unshakable ones, and *hoe in*. Nothing but steady, persistent labour will win in literature. *Dogged does it*. Why not try your hand on some essays on prairie life—the inwardness and out-wardness of it, treating the subject delicately, analytically, *intimately*, exhaustively, and try your luck with William Briggs. Ten or twelve would make a book. Write on the prairie in all its aspects—by day, by night, in winter and summer, etc., etc., etc. Make each essay about three or four thousand words long and put all the airy fancy and thought into it that you can. Call the whole book *The Northern Silence* and write a title essay on that subject. Don't be in a hurry—write just when you feel in the mood for it.

Here it is two hours later. A Christmas caller came in bringing a *duck* and a box of candy. (Write an essay on "Christmas on the Prairie" for your book!) It's really very hard to give good advice under such circumstances. But I was about through anyhow. Really, I'm in earnest. I think you could do it all right. There are many sentences and ideas in your various letters which could be worked admirably into such a series and if you decide to try it I'll copy them out and send them to you.

I must close now, for another caller has come and I do not expect to have any more spare time till after Xmas. I am enclosing the proof of the review that appeared in *National*. You may keep it. Also, as soon as I can get an envelope to fit it I'll send you a souvenir copy of my "Island Hymn," with music.

The best wishes of the season to you,

Yours very cordially,

L.M. Montgomery. ❄

from *The Green Gables Letters* . . .

The indominable *Anne Shirley*, as the world knows, would be with her creator, Lucy Maud Montgomery, for many, many years to come.

Celebrations at the Jardin de l'enfance

BY MARCEL TRUDEL

Courtesy of the Sproule family

*I*n those days, as I have mentioned, boarding-school pupils stayed over Christmas and went home two or three days later for the holidays. And oh, what a marvel the feast of Christmas was at the Jardin de l'enfance! We began preparing for it in early November with singing exercises. As the time drew nearer, we had all sort of little tasks to keep us busy. Among others, we had to write our parents a letter in English, expressing the season's greetings. The English-speaking world's custom of sending Christmas wishes was beginning to spread among French Canadians. Until then, we usually sent New Year's greetings and nothing more. It made sense for us to practise an English custom in the language of the English, and it was also a way of impressing our parents. I don't know why, but instead of going to my adoptive father, this letter had to be sent to my true father, although I no longer had any real contact with him. He can't have got much pleasure from a letter written in English, whereas my adoptive father, who had taught me my first English vocabulary, would have been very proud to receive it.

We also had to prepare the *crèches*. The nuns put these little manger scenes everywhere—in the chapel, in every classroom, and at the ends of corridors. We had to cut out cardboard clogs for our "surprises," just in case the little Jesus (it was not then Pere Noël or Father Christmas) happened to pass through the dormitory. It was early to bed for us on Christmas eve, and we awoke to the sound of hand-bells. A mass followed, wonderfully candle-lit, where we sang in harmony. We went down to the dining hall for the reveillon, and at each place was fruit, cake, and candy. After this we went back to bed. Next morning we found, under each bed, a little cardboard clog filled with good things to eat, placed there by unknown hands. ❉

from *Memoirs of a Less Travelled Road: A Historian's Life*, translated by Jane Brierley

Marcel Trudel's adopted family encouraged him to go into the priesthood, but he decided otherwise, and Canada gained a noted historian. Appointed the first professor of history at Laval University in 1947, Trudel embarked upon his ten-volume *History of New France*. His honours include the Order of Canada and Knight of the National Order of Quebec.

Courtesy of Nancy Moulton

How Santa Claus Came to Cape St. Anthony

BY WILFRED GRENFELL

CAPE ST. ANTHONY, NORTHERN TIP OF NEWFOUNDLAND ABOUT 1892

Early in December we had been dumped from the little mail steamer on the harbour ice about half a mile from shore, and hauled up to the little Mission hospital, where we were to make our headquarters for the winter. The name of our harbour was St. Anthony. Christmas was close upon us. The prospect of enjoying the conventional pleasures of the season was not bright. Not unnaturally our thoughts went over the sea to the family gathering at home, at which our places would be vacant. We should miss the holly and mistletoe, the roast beef and plum pudding, the inevitable crackers, and the giving and receiving of presents, which had always seemed essential to a full enjoyment of the Christmas holiday.

We soon found that few of the children here had ever possessed a toy; and that there was scarcely a single girl that owned a doll. Now and again one would see, nailed high up on the wall, well out of reach of the children, a flimsy, cheaply painted doll; and the mother would explain that her "Pa had got un from a trader, sir, for thirty cents. No, us don't allow Nellie to have it, 'feared lest she might spoil un"—a fear I found to be only too well grounded when I came to examine its anatomy more closely.

Christmas trees in plenty grew near the hospital; and we could easily arrange for a "Father Christmas." The only question was, whether our stock of toys would justify us in inviting so many children as would want to come. It is easy to satisfy children like these, however, and so we announced that we expected Santa Claus on a certain day. There was great talk about the affair. Whispers reached us that Aunt Mary thought her Joe weren't too big to come; sure, he'd be only sixteen. May White was only going eighteen, and she would so like to come. Old Daddy Gilliam would like to sit in a corner. He'd never seen a Christmas tree, and he was nigh on eighty. We were obliged to yield, and with guilty consciences expected twice as many as the room would hold. All through the day before the event the Sister was busy making buns; and it was even whispered that a barrel of apples had been carried over to the "Room."

In the evening a sick call carried me north to a tiny place on the Straits of Belle Isle, where a woman lay in great pain, and by all accounts dying. The dogs were in great form, and travelling was fair enough till we came to a great arm of the sea, which lay right in our path, and was only recently caught over with young ice. To reach the other shore we had to make a wide detour, bumping our way along the rough edge of the old standing ice. Even here the salt water came up through the snow, and the dogs sank to their shoulders in a cold mush that made each mile into half a dozen. We began to think that our chance of getting back in time on the morrow was small indeed. We were also wondering that it seemed to be a real disappointment to ourselves that we should miss the humble attempt at Christmas-keeping.

One thing went a long way toward reconciling us to the disappointment. The case we had come to see proved to be one in which skilled help was of real service. So we were a contented company round the log fire in the little hut, as we sat listening to stories from one and another of the neighbours, who, according to custom, had dropped in to see the stranger. Before long my sleeping bag was loudly calling to me after the exercise of the day. "We must be off by dawn, Uncle Phil, for there's no counting these short days, and we have promised to see that Santa Claus is in time for the Christmas tree tomorrow night at St. Anthony." Soon, stretched out on the floor, we slept as soundly as in a feather bed.

Only a few minutes seemed to have passed when, "'Twill be dawning shortly, Doctor," in the familiar tones of my driver's voice, came filtering into my bag. "Right you are, Rube; put the kettle on and call the dogs; I will be ready in a couple of shakes."

Oh, what a glorious morning! An absolute stillness, and the air as sweet as sugar. Everywhere a mantle of perfect white below, a fathomless depth of cloudless blue overhead—and the first radiance of the coming day blending one into the other with a rich, transparent red. The bracing cold made one feel twenty years younger. We found it a hard job to tackle up the dogs, they were so mad to be off. As we topped the first hill the great bay lay below us, and my driver gave a joyous shout. "Hurrah, Doctor! There's a lead for us." Far out on the ice he had spied a black speck moving toward the opposite shore. A *komatik* had ventured over the young ice, and to follow it would mean a saving of five miles to us.

We made a good landing and scaled the opposite hill, and were galloping over the high barrens when the dogs began to give tongue, loudly announcing that a team was coming from the opposite direction. As we drew near, a muffled figure jumped off, and, hauling his dogs to one side, shouted the customary, "What cheer?"

Then a surprise, "The Doctor, as I live! You're the very man I'm after. Why, there's *komatiks* gone all over the country after you. A lad had shot hisself down at St. Ronald's, and he's bleeding shocking."

"All right, Jake, old friend. The turn for the path is off the big pond, is it not?"

"That's it, Doctor, but I'm coming along anyhow, 'feared I *might* be wanted."

My little leader must have overheard this conversation, for she simply flew over the hills. Yet it was already dusk when at length we shot down the semi-precipice on the side of which the little house clings like a barnacle. The anxious crowd, gathered to await our arrival, disappeared before the avalanche, like a morning mist when the sun rises. Following directions, I found myself in a tiny, naked room, already filled with well-meaning visitors, though they were able to do nothing but look on and defile what little air made its way in through the fixed windows. Fortunately, for want of putty, air leaked in around the glasses.

Stretched on the floor behind the stove lay a pale-faced boy of about ten years. His clothes had been taken off, and an old patchwork quilt covered his body. His right thigh was covered with a heterogeneous mass of bloody rags. Sitting by him was his mother, her forehead resting in her hands as if she were wrestling with some inscrutable problem. She rose as I entered, and without waiting for questions, broke out with: "'Tis Clem, Doctor. He got Dick here to give him the gun to try and shoot a gull, and there were a high ballicater of ice in the way, and he were trying to climb up over it, and he pushed the gun before him with bar'l turned t'wards hisself, and she went off and shot him, and us doesn't know what to do next—next, and—"

While she ran on with her story I cleared the room of visitors, and, kneeling down by the boy, removed the dirty mass of rags that had been used to staunch the blood. The charge had entered the thigh at close quarters above the knee, and passed downwards, blowing the kneecap to pieces. Most of it had passed out again. The loose fragments of bone still adhering to the ragged flesh, the fragments of clothing blown into it, and the foul smell and discoloration added by the gunpowder made the outlook a very ugly one. Moreover, there rose to mind the memory of a similar case in which we had come too late, blood poisoning having set in, and the child having died after much suffering.

The mother had by this time quieted down, and was simply repeating, "What shall us do?"

"There's only one thing to be done. We must pack Clem up and carry him to the hospital right away."

"Iss, Doctor, that's the only way, I'm thinking," she replied. "An' I suppose you'll cut off his leg, and he'll never walk no more, and Oh, dear! What—"

"Come, tear up this calico into strips and bring me some boiling water—mind, it must be well-boiled; and get me that board over there—'twill serve to make a splint; and then go and tell Dick to get the dogs ready at once, for we've a Christmas tree at St. Anthony tonight, and I must be back at all costs."

In this way we kept her too busy to worry or hesitate about letting the child go; for we well knew it was his only chance, and she had never seen a hospital, and the idea of one was as terrifying as a morgue.

"Home, home, home!" to the dogs—and once again our steel runners are humming over the crisp snow. Now in the darkness we are clinging tightly to our hand-ropes as we shoot over the hills. Now the hospital lights are coming up, and now the lights in the windows of the "Room." As we get near they look so numerous and so cheerful that we seem to be approaching a town. Now we can hear the merry ring of children's voices, and can make out a crowd of figures gathered around the doorway. They are waiting for the tardy arrival of "Sandy Claws." Of course, we are at once recognized, and there is a general hush of disappointment as if they had thought at last "Sandy" himself was come.

"He is only a little way behind us," we shouted. "He is coming like a whirl-wind. Look out everybody when he gets here. Don't get too close to his dogs."

Only a little while later, and the barking of dogs announces the approach of the other *komatik*. But we alone are in the secret of its real mission. Some one is calling from the darkness, and a long sleigh with a double-banked team of dogs has drawn up opposite the doorway. Two fur-clad figures, standing by it, steady a huge box which is lashed upon it. The light shining on the near one reveals of his muffled face only two sparkling eyes and large icicles bristling over the muffler from heavy moustache and whiskers, like the ivory tusks of some old bull walrus. Both figures are panting with exertion, and blowing out great clouds of steam like gallop-ing horses on a frosty morning. There could be no doubt about it, this time. Here was the real Sandy Claws at last, come mysteriously over the snows with his dogs and *komatik* and big box and all!

The excitement of the crowd, already intense from anxiety over our own delay, now knew no bounds. Where had they come from? What could be in that big box? How large it looked in the darkness. Could it really been dragged all the way from the North Pole? Luckily, no one had the courage left to go near enough to discover the truth.

The hospital door was swung open, and a loud voice cried out: "Welcome, welcome, Sandy Claws! We're so glad you've come; we thought you'd forgotten us. Come right in. Come right in! Oh, no! don't think of undoing the box outside; why, you'll freeze all those toys out there! Just unlash it and bring it right in as it is. Come in; there's a cup of tea waiting for you before you go over to start your tree growing fruit."

There had been rumors all the week that Sandy Claws would bring his wife this year. There had been whispers even of a baby. So we could explain the second man; for the Eskimo men and women all dress alike in Labrador, which would account for Mrs. Claws' strange taste in clothes. A discreet silence was observed about her frozen whiskers.

A few minutes later another large box was carried over to the "Room." It was full of emptiness, for the toys were on the tree long ago. But two strange masked and bewigged figures stumbled over the snow with it, to carry the little drama to its close. So complete was the faith in the unearthly origin of these our guests that when the curtain went up more than one voice was heard to be calling out for "Ma" and "Dad," while a lad of several summers was found hidden under the seat when it came his turn to go up and get his "prize."

And so Santa Claus came to St. Anthony, and brought a gift for us as well as presents for the children. Indeed, the best was the one he had kept for us, who had so unworthily thought that the outlook for a happy Christmas was but a poor one. Sleeping overhead, in a clean, white cot, free of pain, and with a good fighting chance for his life, lay our bright-faced lad—Clem. The gift to us this Christmas day was the chance to save his life. We would not have exchanged it for any gift we have ever heard of. At the old home, where doctors are plentiful, such a gift were impossible.

The great life-giving gift to the world that Christmas stands for was to be *ours* to thus faintly re-echo on this needy, far-off shore. ❄

from Wilfred Grenfell—His Life and Work

British-born Dr. Wilfred Grenfell came to Canada in 1892, determined to improve the life of the poor. He established hospitals and orphanage-schools in Labrador and northwestern Newfoundland while working as a missionary-doctor, and was knighted for his services in 1927. Sir Wilfred died in 1940.

Christmas at the Sour Dough Hotel

BY ANDREW CRUICKSHANK

Courtesy of the Dawson City Museum and Historical Society, 984.1.107, The Isaac Collection

My Very Dear Doe,

Here we are the day after Christmas. Oh how I thought of you all during the past two days, all the little incidents of Christmases long past came to me as it were a pageant. Gee how happy we all were and what wonderful times we had.

My Christmas was a very uneventful one, nothing much happened. On Christmas eve we had a good dinner in the barracks, composed of oyster soup, roast turkey and all the good things that go with it, then plum pudding and brandy sauce, mince pies, jam tarts, cakes, fruit and liquor, certainly a fine feed and excellently cooked. Of course we had a few little speeches and all was friendly and fine. The dinner over at 9:00 p.m. left us wondering what on earth to do. Some sat down to read, some to write, some to play the phonograph and drink. Tidd and I felt like doing none of these things, so we changed into outside clothes and stepped into the night, which was forty degrees below with a dirty wind and fine snow. There were no friendly stars, no smiling glow from the northern lights, nothing to show us that we had any friends. We walked five or six miles, then turned back and talked over Christmases of long ago. When we got back we turned in and never woke until Christmas day. I did stables at 6:30 a.m., had a little fruit and bacon and eggs for breakfast then lay on my bed and read. In the afternoon I went with the orchestra to the hospital to help give a little music to the patients. In the evening four of us went down town to a restaurant to dinner and I had a dandy feed. On arriving home Tidd and I played and sang until 10:30 p.m. and then turned in. ❄

from *Spirit of the Yukon*

Andrew Cruickshank joined the Royal Canadian Mounted Police, and in 1924 he was sent to Dawson City. Three years later he decided to start Yukon Airlines. Cruickshank's *Queen of the Yukon* landed in Whitehorse on October 25, 1927.

The Freeport Angel BY RITA MOIR

FREEPORT, NEAR YARMOUTH, NOVA SCOTIA 1991

*W*e have a dark spruce, cut from the hilltop over the bay, but we have no Freeport angel.

We have a painted goose egg and bits of seashell, Christmas tree lights and gold rivets on string, but our tree needs an angel.

Andy heads for his workshop, Chris for her sewing basket, and I tinker for trinkets.

We meet back at the kitchen table and on the blue checkered tablecloth make our own angel.

The Freeport angel is carved from white styrofoam, the kind discarded in the bay. Her eyes are green glass broken and rolled smooth on the tides below the fish plant, the skin drooping over her wizened right eye, her hair red yarn, shoulder-length, parted strictly down the middle, spraying out over earrings of yellow-breasted toucans perched on tropical leaves. The southern birds gaze along her rouged cheekbones up to her emerald eyes. Her face is flat, her eyebrows pencilled, lips a thin smile that has tasted the oceans from Buenos Aires to the Bay of Fundy, the old sea-trading routes, rum and fish and bolts of cloth—her dress a faded patchwork that still lifts some spark from her hair.

The Freeport angel is Pippi Longstocking gone to sea, her father long dead, she is middle-aged now, her chinline broad and flattened, we can still see her hair in pigtails, Pippi on the beach, Pippi lost, Pippi fighting pirates, Pippi finding home again.

The Freeport angel is not made of straw, she is not angelic, she does not glow or shine through fine-spun angel's hair, she is not pastel. She sits on a bow of dark island spruce, tough as the island wind, she is a lookout on a spar. She is red and green and black, framed by red lights like beacons saying you're almost home. ❄

from *Survival Gear*

Minnesota-born author and journalist Moir (1952–), who lives in the BC Kootenays, drew upon her experiences of a year in the fishing community of Freeport, Digby County, Nova Scotia, for this first memoir of travel and personal discovery.

Courtesy of John Sproule

Christmas Parade BY MARSHA BOULTON

HOLSTEIN, ONTARIO 2000

*I*n rural communities, if a town is large enough to have a Main Street, you can bet that it has a Santa Claus parade. This tradition usually involves giant transport trailer trucks, fire engines, police cars with intrusive sirens, and tractors trimmed with Christmas lights. Drum majorettes strut and men in skirts play Christmas carols on sheep bladders. The grand finale is St. Nick himself, and the whole thing ends in a rage of shopping that warms the hearts of the members of the local Chamber of Commerce.

But in one southwestern Ontario village, there is a distinctly different parade. No lights, no sirens, no fossil-fuel fumes, no commercials, and nowhere much to shop afterward.

Instead, Holstein, Ontario, 100 km northwest of Toronto, hosts a non-mechanized Santa Claus parade featuring the clip clop of homemade, horse-drawn floats and cutters, and the vocal charms of local choirs. There are no razzle-dazzle bands, but a gaggle of children play "Joy to the World" and other seasonal favourites on multi-coloured plastic kazoos.

The whole parade lasts less than an hour. At the end, free hot dogs are served at the pavilion in the village park, where a child-oriented Snofest features such activities as wreath-tossing and photo sessions with Santa.

When sleigh bells ring in Holstein, everybody listens. Six years ago, when the first old-fashioned Christmas parade marched down the road past the Holstein General Store and Feed Mill, it was primarily local people who clawed their way through a December fog to watch the horses go by and to wave to friends who festooned pony carts and hay wagons with homemade nativity scenes and garland-wrapped trees.

But word has spread about this homespun, environmentally friendly parade. For the past couple of Christmases, several thousand visitors have lined along the 1.5-km parade route. And for urbanites who come from Kitchener, Guelph, Collingwood and, yes, even Toronto, it is quite overwhelming.

It is not uncommon to see tears well up in middle-aged eyes.

Last year's parade featured nearly 50 animal-powered entries, including two teams of miniature horses, one donkey, two cows and an unidentified number of dogs wearing reindeer ears.

There is nothing overtly pretentious about the parade—cedar bows on wagons are often affixed with duct tape—but the sentiment is sincere, genuine, and infectious.

"People pass each other on the sidewalk saying 'Merry Christmas,' and everybody is smiling or singing," marvelled University of Guelph professor Nancy Ellwand.

As second-time visitors, Ellwand's three children were so captivated that they wanted to be a part of the parade. Kazoo Band organizer Dinah Christie happily accommodated their mother's request.

"There's a lot of leeway in this parade," says actor-singer Christie, who has a farm nestled in the rolling hills surrounding the village. "Besides, you don't have to know much about music to play the kazoo—as Bacall said to Bogart: 'You just put your lips together and blow.'"

Seventy-year-old Lyle Rawn has been in the parade from the beginning, along with his grey Percherons, Bud and Duke. He prepares the horses by taking them for long sleigh rides across the fields of the family farm on the outskirts of the village.

The day before the parade, he brings "the boys" into his heated shed and washes their white manes and tails until they gleam.

"I don't have fancy show harnesses, but I like them to look good," says Rawn, who is by no means the oldest driver in the parade. His 76-year-old cousin, Russell, brings a team of chestnut and cream Belgian horses.

The hooves of the big draft horses are the size of pie plates, and they clomp along the snow-covered route guided by seasoned drivers who like nothing better than to show off their gentle giants. There is even an eight-horse mounted choir, whose songs are interspersed with the occasional whinny.

The whole extravaganza costs less than $1,500 to produce, with horse owners providing their fancy-dressed rigs at their own expense and the local Boy Scouts stuffing goody bags for the kids.

"Everyone pitches in, and it seems to bring out the best in people," admits organizer Erika Matheson, who taps volunteer resources from nearly all of the 117 families in the village.

"It's special, all right," confides Lyle Rawn. "And you know why? I think it's because the horses like the parade as much as the people do." ❄

from *Letters from the Country: Omnibus*

Marsha Boulton, a former urban dweller who traded heels for wellington boots, hung on to her sense of humour and chronicled her rural adventures.

Courtesy of Nancy Moulton

The Trapper's Christmas Eve BY ROBERT SERVICE

KLONDIKE, YUKON

It's mighty lonesome-like and drear.
Above the Wild the moon rides high,
And shows up sharp and needle-clear
The emptiness of earth and sky;
No happy homes with love aglow;
No Santa Claus to make believe;
Just snow and snow, and then more snow;
It's Christmas Eve, it's Christmas Eve.

And here I am where all things end,
And Undesirables are hurled;
A poor old man without a friend,
Forgot and dead to all the world;
Clean out of sight and out of mind . . .
Well, maybe it is better so;
We all in life our level find,
And mine, I guess, is pretty low.

Yet as I sit with pipe alight
Beside the cabin-fire, it's queer
This mind of mine must take tonight
The backward trail of fifty year.
The schoolhouse and the Christmas tree;
The children with their cheeks aglow;
Two bright blue eyes that smile on me . . .

Just half a century ago.
Again (it's maybe forty years),
With faith and trust almost divine,
These same blue eyes, abrim with tears,
Through depths of love look into mine,
A parting, tender, soft, and low;
With arms that cling and lips that cleave . . .
Ah me! It's all so long ago,
Yet seems so sweet this Christmas Eve.

Just thirty years ago, again . . .
We say a bitter last goodbye;
Our lips are white with wrath and pain;
Our little children cling and cry.
Whose was the fault? It matters not,
For men and woman both deceive;
It's buried now and all forgot,
Forgiven, too, this Christmas Eve.

And she (God pity me) is dead;
Our children men and women grown,
I like to think that they are wed,
With little children of their own,
That crowd around their Christmas tree . . .
I would not ever have them grieve,
Or shed a single tear for me,
To mar their joy this Christmas Eve.

Stripped to the buff and gaunt and still
Lies all the land in grim distress.
Like lost soul wailing, long and shrill,
A wolf-howl cleaves the emptiness.
Then hushed as Death is everything.
The moon rides haggard and forlorn . . .
"O hark the herald angels sing!"
God bless all men—it's Christmas morn.

from *The Collected Poems of Robert Service*

The Bard of the Yukon, Robert Service lived in the Yukon for only eight years; before he left, his poems of the North had become world-renowned.

The Front-Room BY NELLIE MCCLUNG

NEAR BRANDON, MANITOBA 1880S

The front-room always got a new coat of whitewash on the log walls at Christmas, and everything was scoured as white as sand or soap could make it. The hand-knit lace curtains, brought from Ontario, were washed and starched and stretched on home-made frames, so they hang straight and reach the floor. Short curtains were considered slightly indecent. The two long widths of rag carpet in bright stripes with orange warp were brought out and laid on the white floor, with the good mats, one hooked and one braided. The home-made lounge had a covering of dark maroon canton flannel and was well supplied with patchwork cushions, crazy patterns of silks and satins and two log cabins, one made of "stuff pieces," the other one of prints. There were two bookcases made with spools, painted black, and set with shelves, and a "what-not" of five shelves, on which stood china ornaments, a shell box, with a green plush pincushion on the top, apples filled with cloves, and cups of saucers, (honourably retired from active service because of crack, or missing handles, but with these defects tactfully concealed in the way they were placed), coloured glass mugs, and on the top, a bouquet of prairie grasses, set in a frosted-glass vase, a lace pattern on deep blue. I remember it well, for I broke it years later, when bouncing a ball, on the floor. Who would have thought a yarn ball would bounce so high?

When the weather got cold, the kitchen stove had to be brought into the big room, and it was a family grief when this change had to be made. If the weather did not come down too hard, the stove was kept out until after Christmas. Later, when the storm doors and windows were added, and a bigger heater bought, a fine big barrel of a stove, with a row of mica windows around its middle, through which the coals glowed with all the colours of a sunset, the kitchen stove remained in the kitchen all winter.

But even when the kitchen stove was in the middle of the big room, there was a cheerful roominess about it. The woodbox papered with pictures of the Ice Palace in Montreal (*Family Herald Supplement*), when covered with two boards over which a quilt was spread, made a nice warm seat, and when we got the hanging lamp from Brandon, with a pale pink shade on which a brown deer poised for a leap across a chasm through which a green stream dashed in foam on the rocks, the effects was magical, and in the pink light the whitewashed walls were softened into alabaster.

We had two new pictures now, enlarged photographs of father and mother in heavy oak frames with a gilt edge, done by a travelling artist who drove a team of mules and carried a few lines of tinware. Every family in the neighbourhood had taken advantage of his easy plan to secure a lasting work of art. You paid only for the frame and received the picture entirely free, though the offer might be withdrawn any minute for he was doing this merely to get his work known. He said there was no nicer way to give one's parents a pleasant surprise, and the pictures would be delivered in time for Christmas. When they came, we all had a surprise. We had thought that the seven dollars and thirty-five cents paid for both frames, but we were wrong. Each one cost that amount, and even at that the artist was losing money. The pictures were accepted and hung on the log walls, and in the declivities behind them were kept tissue-paper patterns, newspaper clippings, and other semi-precious documents, thus relieving the congestion in the real archives, lodged in the lower regions of the clock, where notes, grain-tickets, and tax receipts were kept. ❄

from *Nellie McClung: The Complete Autobiography: Clearing in the West & The Stream Runs Fast*

Born in Ontario, Nellie Mooney moved with her family to Manitoba when she was seven years old. At 16, she taught school in rural Manitoba, where she later became interested in social and health problems caused by alcohol. She married Robert McClung in 1916, and the couple had five children. One of Canada's first feminists, Nellie McClung was a fierce supporter of the women's vote, a right won in 1916. After the family moved to Edmonton, Alberta, she served as a Liberal member of the Legislative Assembly for one term, while keeping up her prolific writing career and her interests in political and social issues.

The Indians' Christmas Tree BY MALI QUELQUELTALKO

ALL HALLOWS ANGLICAN SCHOOL, YALE, BRITISH COLUMBIA DECEMBER 18, 1889

Rev. and Dear Sir,

The Sister Superior told me to try and write you a letter about the most interesting things I could think of. I think the most interesting thing to us just now is the Indians' Christmas tree.

The Sisters did not know what to do for the Indians this Christmas; they had no woollen scarves or pretty handkerchiefs, because not any had been sent out to them as usual by the good English people.

Then Sister Superior said on Sunday, "We will light the tree with Chinese lanterns and hang on it buns and jam tarts, and tin mugs and brew a can of hot coffee, and stand it underneath the tree." Then everyone laughed, and thought it would be nice about the coffee and tarts, but not to put them on the tree. Afterwards Miss H., our governess, said, "Let everyone who can work make three things for the Indians' tree." So we are all set to work, and we are all so busy we have almost forgotten our own school party, but our tree is the Sisters' secret; we never see it until the last minute, and then, oh! It is so beautiful, and we always have such nice good times.

Now I have thought of another thing that is interesting. There are two old Indian men here, and the white people think they are exactly alike, but they are no relation to each other. Three years ago they were baptized, and George, the Indian interpreter, and one of the Sisters were witnesses. The old men were called by new names; one was Thomas and one was David. When they came out of Church, somehow they got mixed up, and Sister and George did not agree which was Thomas and which was David. The old men laughed so; they didn't know anything about English names, but are glad to be Christians. Now Sister has made two nice warm caps for them, and she says she wants Thomas to have the one with fur, and David one with red wool; but she says as they always get mixed up, she will put "David" on the fur, and "Thomas" on the wool cap, and then she is sure the right old men will get them. We hope it will be a nice snowy Christmas week, and we shall be able to have a sleigh ride to the little schoolhouse by the Parsonage for the Indians' party.

We want a new schoolhouse very badly. It is very pretty where we now live, nearly a mile from the Church, and we have more rooms than in the old house, but it is not large enough for us all. Sister is always telling people that we have no room for more children. The Sisters went out begging last spring, and got $1,500 to build, but it is not enough, and we have to wait until someone will send us more money.

I hope I have not written a too long letter.

Mali Quelqueltalka ❄

from the *Diocese of New Westminster, Vol. 1, 1889-1896*

Mali was a sixteen-year-old native child who learned English during her four years at this Anglican residential school on the banks of the Fraser River.

Almanac BY LAMBERT DE BOILIEU

BATTLE HARBOUR, LABRADOR 1850S

Sincere Christmas Greetings and Best Wishes for the New Year

Courtesy of the Sproule Family

*I*t is at Christmas-day that the old hands make their almanacs. I can best explain how this is done by giving the information as I received it: "Why, you see," said an old fellow, "I've got this 'ere board, and makes my almanac upon that. I divides the first day after Christmas into four parts, and takes notes of the quarter the wind blows from, and makes my observations on the same, and calls that January—each quarter o' the day representing a week; and I do the same up to the sixth of January, being twelve days after Christmas. I consider them there twelve days represents the twelve months of the year, and as I have made these almanacs for forty years and have always found them true, you can laugh as much as you like." I must confess the owner of this almanac was always an authority as to how the summer would turn out, the time the coast would be clear of ice, what sort of fall it would be, etc. I visited the old man's quarters, and there I found, transferred from his board to the side of his room, sundry queer hieroglyphics which he said he understood well himself, and which I daresay he did. Coupled with wolf's-head, this primitive way of rivalling Murphy* some impressed me: at all events, I have seen enough to know that only fools laugh at the simple lore of old folk.

*P. Murphy, Esq. Under the date of 20 Jan. he said, "Fair, prob. lowest deg. of winter temp." By a happy chance this proved to be a remarkably cold day, the thermometer at sunrise standing at four degrees below zero . . . the shop of his publishers, Messrs. Whittaker & Co., was besieged with customers, while the winter 1837–8 became known as Murphy's winter. The 1838 almanac ran to forty-five editions, and the prophet made 3,000 £, which he almost immediately lost in an unsuccessful speculation in corn.

from *Recollections of Labrador Life*

As a young Englishman, Lambert de Boilieu sailed to Labrador to take charge of the business interests of the British company for which he worked. He kept a detailed journal of local customs and the people he met.

Coyote Carols BY DICK FAIRFAX

C hristmas came and we both got parcels from home. We were also invited for Christmas dinner by the storekeeper in town. But the weather man had his plans too. On Christmas Eve a blizzard started and lasted for three days. The cold was really intense. Snow sifted right into the shack. We had previously put poles sawed in two as markers between the stable and the spring otherwise we should have had difficulty in watering the horses. A huge drift formed between the shack and the stables. These were truly Arctic conditions.

For Christmas dinner we had roast beef and frozen potatoes. A box of candied fruit in a dainty box looked strangely out of place on the bare home-made table. The pudding from home was the main item on the menu. We ate the whole pudding. No use saving any for next day to warm up, it would freeze overnight anyway. After sunset on Christmas Day the wind went down a bit. I went outside and called Bill to come and listen to the carols. "Coyotes," said Bill, "in excellent voice." For a while we listened and I'm sure both of us were thinking of home. But it was no weather for standing around in reveries. We went inside, fired up the stove, and left the frigid weather to the coyotes. ❄

from *So Soon Forgotten*—a young English pioneer's diary of home-steading in western Canada from 1904 to 1925

The Teddy Bear Coat BY HESTA MACDONALD

PRINCE EDWARD ISLAND 1930s

T he most visible sign of "hard times," for me at least, was the clothing that I wore during my childhood Depression Days. Our house was warm and dry; good food was plentiful, and we had electricity, a telephone, and a car. Clothing seven children, however, was an expensive matter, and since I was the youngest of three girls, I wore mostly hand-me-down clothes. I never lacked warm underwear, good hand-knit mittens, and wool overstockings. Ankle-length shoes were half-soled by my father. I can still see him, bent over the iron shoe last, his mouth holding the little shoe tacks which he patiently pounded one by one around the rim of the stout leather sole. He had a little tack hammer that was never used except for shoe repair.

Like most of the children in my rural community, I had two dresses which alternated for school wear. As soon as I got home from school each day, I changed to an older, more-worn dress for work and play. There was also a "best" dress for Sunday or to be worn on very special occasions. Two of my classmates had three aunts who were nurses in Boston. These little girls always had lots of pretty dresses!

I didn't have an aunt to bring me new dresses, but I was fortunate to have a dear grand aunt who was skillful with needle and thread. She was an octogenarian who visited our home for a couple of weeks twice a year, and for me those were the best times of the year. Aunt Annie's hands were always busy, and whenever she was at our home she busied herself with renovating clothing for me—letting down hems, or taking a tuck here and there to make somebody else's dress fit me.

Making my grandmother's worn-out coat into one for me was quite a task. First, all the seams of the old coat were ripped out, and the material was carefully washed and pressed. Meanwhile Aunt Annie made a coat pattern in my diminutive size from an old *Halifax Mail* newspaper. Then the material salvaged from grandmother's coat was turned, giving a new lease on life to the ugly gray-green woolen material. My mother did her best to relieve the drabness of my "new" coat by having Aunt Annie line it with new pink paisley flannelette, and I really did try not to let on how much I hated that coat. I didn't grow very fast, so I wore that ugly coat for two years.

Then came the winter that I was ten years old, and a wonderful thing came about in my wardrobe. How my mother chanced to get a catalogue from the United States I know not, but she sent an order for the most beautiful coat for me. I had never had a new coat in my life. Mine! All mine! Even better, it was a "Teddy Bear" coat, a very popular coast in that era. The material was a soft plush fake fur in a delicate cinnamon brown colour! My parents impressed upon me that this was my Christmas present, although I could wear it in the cold weeks of autumn. Christmas present indeed— I wanted nothing more.

Sometimes it seems that life can be cruel. Over the next year, I had my growth spurt, and when that came, my beautiful "Teddy Bear" coat was far too small. Ironically, my mother sold it for $5, half of its original price, to our next-door neighbour whose little girl was three years younger than I was. All that winter, as I returned to wearing somebody's remodelled coat, I had to watch Vivian proudly wearing the beautiful cinnamon "Teddy Bear." ❄

from *Voice for Island Seniors*—reminiscences of earlier times from Prince Edward Island's seniors

Moving Day BY UNA PATIENCE CARLSON

BURNABY, BRITISH COLUMBIA 1920

*D*ec. 25, 1920. Christmas Day. What a time to arrive in a new province, new municipality, and a new home! Dad had sold his farm in Saskatchewan in order to move to the land of his dreams, British Columbia, which he had visited sometime before getting married.

He wanted to provide a better home and education for his family, something other than what he could foresee: grain crops plagued with grasshoppers, rust, drought, and so on. He had come to the West Coast before us to find a place to settle.

Imagine his dilemma when Mother wired that our family doctor had advised her to leave my grandmother's place in Saskatchewan as a cousin there might be developing diphtheria, which would quarantine the entire household, including us.

Poor Dad! He had to find a house immediately, move the furniture and be ready for the arrival of his wife and five children in a matter of days rather than weeks. So he bought the property at 240–15th Avenue, the houses then being numbered from New Westminster and not from Vancouver.

The house, located in the area now known as East Burnaby, hadn't been lived in for years. A broken window in one of the upstairs rooms had allowed the neighborhood pigeons to usurp it for a dovecote.

My brother, Wallace, and I were old enough to be saddened at the thought of leaving relatives and friends behind, but also excited at the adventures which lay ahead, even though we wouldn't know a single soul in our new, far-away western home.

Three things I'll always remember—the CNR train crawling across the Fraser River on the lower level of the double-decker bridge at New Westminster on a very grey morning, coming to a stop at the bleak station nestled at the bottom of a big earth bank with little vegetation; Dad waiting happily to greet us, wearing a sprig of cedar in his lapel; and the joy of climbing into the familiar 1917 Maxwell touring car and taking off up the Second Street hill towards our new home.

Other than the folks at the railway depot, we didn't see another person until we reached Third Avenue, when we spotted Santa Claus walking towards downtown. The familiar figure cheered us up, especially as there hadn't been the usual anticipation nor any Christmas Eve excitement on the train. Dad assured us that Christmas 1921 would be different. ❄

from *Pioneer Tales of Burnaby*—a collection of stories about Burnaby's early days

The Christmas Cake That Never Was

BY EVELYN JOHNSON

SIX NATIONS RESERVE, NEAR BRANTFORD, ONTARIO ABOUT 1875

Pauline Johnson. Photograph taken on Christmas day.
Courtesy of Raymond Skye

*I*t was decided one year that Pauline should make our Christmas cake. She was just a young girl, in her early 'teens. It fell to my lot to prepare many of the ingredients. All the raisins had to be stoned; the peel had to be cut, and the currants washed and dried. The night before the cake was to be baked, I made those preparations. Next day about ten o'clock, Pauline began making her Christmas cake. It took several hours to bake in two large pans. About 7.30 that evening, mother and Pauline went to the kitchen to examine the cakes, which they thought had baked long enough. They turned them out of the pans to cool. A currant which stuck to the pan mother put into her mouth. "It is very hot," she said. Pauline said, "Of course it is; it's just out of the oven." And took herself upstairs to her room. When she had gone, mother broke off a small piece of the cake and tasted it and then called my sisters. They found that Pauline had used two teaspoons of cayenne pepper instead of two of ground mace. Needless to say, we had no Christmas cake that year. ❄

from *Buckskin & Broadcloth: A Celebration of E. Pauline Johnson— Tekahionwake 1861–1913*—reminiscences of Mohawk poet and writer Pauline Johnson's sister, Evelyn, as told to author Sheila M.F. Johnston

'Grannie's' Christmas Dinner BY GEORGE C.F. PRINGLE

DAWSON, YUKON 1904

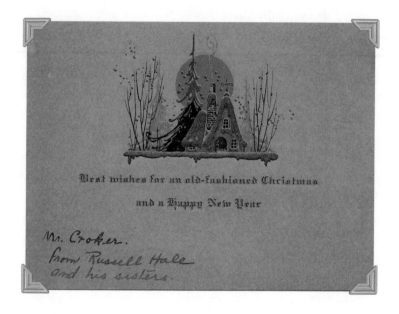

Best wishes for an old-fashioned Christmas
and a Happy New Year

Mr. Croker.
from Russell Hale
and his sisters.

Courtesy of Raymond Skye

*I*t was the winter of 1904, Jas. McAllister had invited me to have dinner on Christmas Day with him and his wife. Their cabin was half-way up the mountain side on the left limit of Hunker Creek, six miles below Gold Bottom camp where I lived. It was "fifty below" that morning.

Breakfast finished and the dishes washed, I put on my parka over my other clothes and with fur gauntlets and moccasins I was ready for the road. First I went across to Bill Lennox's cabin and asked him to feed my dogs at noon. Then I hit the trail for McAllister's.

It was towards noon before I turned out of the main trail, taking one that wound its way up the mountainside for half a mile until it came out on a flat stretch of snow. I was now above the frost-fog and could see, a few hundred yards away, a small straight plume of white smoke rising out of what looked like a big shapely snowdrift. The trail ran straight to it and soon I could see a log or two of the little cabin showing between the comb of snow hanging from the eves and the snow banked up against the base. The door was low and when it opened in response to my knock I had to bow my head to get in. I entered without ceremony for they were expecting me. I heard a cheery voice with a Doric accent tell me to "come right in." I could hear the voice but could see no one for with the opening of the door the warm air met the cold and immediately formed a veil of mist. But it was only a moment for in the North, in winter, you don't keep the door open long. You either come in or get out, as the case may be, without lingering on the threshold.

But what a hearty welcome when the door was shut behind me from McAllister and his good wife! There was something special about their welcome too, even in the hospitable north. To the miners generally I was known as the "sky-pilot," or "parson," or by my first or last name. But to these two old Presbyterians with their Scottish traditions I was always "the minister," and so in my reception there was a respect and courtesy that gave their greetings a rare fineness of tone. Sometimes it is good for you to have people place you on a pedestal. You usually try to measure up to expectations and in that country self-respect was often the sheet-anchor that kept you from drifting to the devil.

It was only a one-room cabin eight feet wide and twelve feet long, log walls chinked with moss, rough board floor, roof of poles covered with a foot of moss and a half foot of earth on the top. The only place I could stand upright in it was under the ridge-pole. There was one window of four panes, each about the size of a woman's handkerchief. The glass was coated an inch deep in frost, but some light came through, though not enough to dispense with candles. Under the window was a table, simply a shelf two and a half feet wide and three feet long. At the end of the cabin opposite the door was the bed, and to the left the stove, a sheet-iron one-chambered affair with an oven in the pipe, a simple, small, Klondike stove which was not much to look at capable of great things when rightly handled. After taking off my parka it was to the stove I went first. It's a habit you form in the North anyway, but if you have a moustache, as I had, the heavy icicles formed by your breath on a six-mile mile walk in that extreme cold need to be thawed off near the stove, and that by a gentle, careful process, the reason for this gentleness only experience would make you appreciate. Once this is done there is no need to sit near the stove. Indeed you can't get far away from it if you stay in the cabin.

But I must describe my host and hostess. Mr. and Mrs. McAllister looked more like brother and sister than husband and wife. They were both small of stature and resembled each other. Both were well past middle life. Their hair was growing gray. They had no children, but his pet name for his little woman was "Grannie." McAllister had graduated from a Scottish university and after his marriage decided to leave the old land for America. As the years went on they found themselves getting within sight

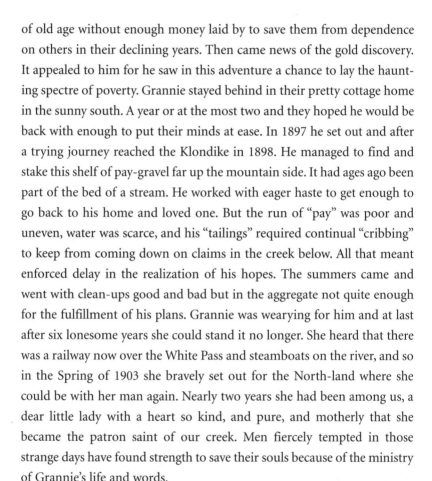

of old age without enough money laid by to save them from dependence on others in their declining years. Then came news of the gold discovery. It appealed to him for he saw in this adventure a chance to lay the haunting spectre of poverty. Grannie stayed behind in their pretty cottage home in the sunny south. A year or at the most two and they hoped he would be back with enough to put their minds at ease. In 1897 he set out and after a trying journey reached the Klondike in 1898. He managed to find and stake this shelf of pay-gravel far up the mountain side. It had ages ago been part of the bed of a stream. He worked with eager haste to get enough to go back to his home and loved one. But the run of "pay" was poor and uneven, water was scarce, and his "tailings" required continual "cribbing" to keep from coming down on claims in the creek below. All that meant enforced delay in the realization of his hopes. The summers came and went with clean-ups good and bad but in the aggregate not quite enough for the fulfillment of his plans. Grannie was wearying for him and at last after six lonesome years she could stand it no longer. She heard that there was a railway now over the White Pass and steamboats on the river, and so in the Spring of 1903 she bravely set out for the North-land where she could be with her man again. Nearly two years she had been among us, a dear little lady with a heart so kind, and pure, and motherly that she became the patron saint of our creek. Men fiercely tempted in those strange days have found strength to save their souls because of the ministry of Grannie's life and words.

But we were just sitting down to dinner at the little table in front of the window. First I said a simple grace, thanking God for our food and asking a blessing upon it and us. We had soup to begin with, thick hot Scotch broth it was, then roast ptarmigan, two each of these plump, tasty little birds which the old man had shot from the cabin door, native cranberry sauce, parsnips and potatoes. These were good "cheechako spuds" shipped in from the South. We had home-grown potatoes in the Klondike sometimes, but in a summer which had one or two nights of nipping frost every month it was hard to ripen them. They were usually small and green, and so "wet" that the saying was "you had to wear a bathing-suit to eat them." Also of course there was home-made bread and excellent tea.

But the dessert was the masterpiece of the meal. It was a good, hot, Canadian blueberry pie about as big round as the top of a piano-stool. It had a top crust on it and the juice was bubbling out through the little slits. It certainly looked delicious and it tasted the same. It was cut into only four pieces. I maintain that no self-respecting pie should be cut into more than four pieces except perhaps in the case of a very large family. Grannie gave me one piece, McAllister one, and took one herself. That left one over and when I was through with my piece I was urged of course to have the other piece. What could I do? What would you have done in my place? Courtesy, inclination to oblige, and my palate all said take. My waistband said "Have a care," but it was awfully good pie and I cleaned the plate.

Then McAllister lit his pipe. Grannie cleared up the table but left the dishwashing until after I had gone as she wanted to share the conversation. What a jolly three hours we had! Not a great deal there to make us happy, you would say; a lonely log-cabin in a far land and in the depth of an almost Arctic winter with no other human habitation within sight or sound. Yet we forgot the fierce cold that circled us, for the little place was comfortable, and better still our hearts were warm with love and friendship. McAllister was finely educated and had travelled, so the cabin was neither small nor lonely. Its walls expanded and took in many guests. A goodly throng was there for we wandered at will among a world of books and men. He loved a good, clean joke, and let me tell you when we got going the stories, both grave and gay, were worth your hearing.

Grannie was with us heart and soul in it all. Her face beamed with cheeriness and good will. Sometimes, however, a far-away look came into her brown eyes. I knew what it meant. She longed to get away from the North and back again to the sunshine of her Southern home. She was getting on in years and our extreme winters were very trying to her. Whenever she got half a chance she would tell us something about their home in California, the warm, bright summers, the lovely gardens she and her neighbours had, and the flowers growing in profusion, especially the roses charming the eye and filling the air with their perfume.

Dear wee Grannie, she never lived to go back. One winter the brutal cold gripped her and in spite of all we could do it took her life away. It was a sad day when we placed her body in the grave on that hillside. All the creek assembled to show their affection, and in deep sorrow. It was her last request that she should be buried there. She didn't want to be far from the man she loved even though it meant a lonely grave in a lonely land. The Klondike became McAllister's homeland until the end of his days on earth. He died in 1922 and was buried beside his wife on the lonely mountain slope.

But there was no thought of sorrow that Christmas Day. Nowhere in the world was there a merrier party, and when it came time for me to go (I had a wedding at Last Chance Roadhouse), it was with a feeling that the cabin had been a sanctuary of friendship, happiness and hospitality. When I went out into the darkness and the bitter cold I was hardly conscious of it for my heart was aglow.

from *Adventures in Service*

The Reverend George Pringle, who had a log church on Gold Bottom Creek, was a tireless supporter of the Klondike miners. "Nothing was too much trouble for him, and the men loved him," recalled the late Mrs. Lucille Hooker, who grew up in Dawson during the Gold Rush.

The Toy Shop BY JACK PEACH

CALGARY, ALBERTA 1923

B ack in the 1920s and 1930s a large and memorable youthful Christmastide event for children of Calgary's many underfunded families was the annual Toy Shop. It was a joint effort of the Boy Scouts and Girl Guides, the Wolf Cubs, Brownies, and Rovers.

Its instigator was F. Leslie Sara, a manufacturers' representative and scoutmaster of the Tenth Troop in Rideau. He hatched the idea while accompanying the manager of a Calgary department store assessing the post-Christmas, pawed-over remnants of the store's toy department. Sara's enthusiasm for a soiled-toy repairing venture was contagious. Lt. Col. J.H. Woods, publisher of the *Calgary Herald*, was putting together the Herald Sunshine Society, which would sponsor food hampers for local needy families. The idea of adding toys to next year's Christmas hampers fitted in perfectly with his plan.

The Kiwanis Club picked up the idea, too, and supplied tools, hardware, solder, paint, glue, and plaster of Paris, for every kind of toy repair job. As the winter of 1923 approached, the first Toy Shop was organized, housed in the empty former Merchants Bank of Canada building on the southeast corner of Centre Street and Eighth Avenue.

Scores of uniformed young scouts and cubs, as well as guides and brownies manned the workbenches and loaner sewing machines, spending every spare evening and weekend hour refurbishing wind-up toy vehicles, re-wigging dolls, painting, mending, sewing, and rebuilding used playthings.

Each November the Capitol and the Palace movie theatres held a Toy Matinee at which Harold Lloyd, Charlie Chaplin, and Fatty Arbuckle comedy films were shown to packed houses of youngsters. Their admission price was a new toy or one that could be mended.

One of my own vivid Toy Shop memories is of suddenly encountering, on the upper floor of the workplace, an open box of eyes—all staring up at me, each pair vacantly gazing from under obviously false eyelashes. They were spares to be installed by the Girl Guides in damaged sleepy-eyed dolls, which were the rage of that time.

There was no shortage of adult volunteers either. One unemployed man brought a small lathe and operated it there for us. The Crown Lumber Company brought scrap-ends of hardwood for mending coaster wagons. Roy Beavers, manager of the Club Cafe just up the block from the Toy Shop, kept us well supplied with simple meals and snacks, as did Jimmy Condon, who brought tasty treats from his Palace of Eats on the corner of Eighth and First Street West.

The Toy Shop "Santa's helpers" turned out doll houses, dolls, miniature cradles, rocking horses, and marble sets. Games such as checker, Parcheesi, Snakes and Ladders, and Ludo were cannibalized and reassembled in complete sets. Even tricycles and doll carriages were put back on their wheels and repainted almost as good as new.

City-wide, the fire department joined the pre-Christmas activity by letting neighbourhoods know that fire halls should be used as drop-off points from which the toys would be forwarded to the shop.

In those pre-"batteries not included" days, we youngsters, keen to be of help, tackled clockwork and springs, little flywheels, axles and ratchets.

I recall being very eager to please and be useful, a desire hampered only by the fact that I was all thumbs and still pretty sloppy with a paint or enamel brush.

One of my annual last-minute joys was playing assistant to Santa Claus. In his absence on a busy Christmas morning, I had the joyful task of handing out toys to the homeless children at the Salvation Army Booth Memorial Home, which was just a block from where we lived. The boxes of surprise gifts had been dropped off by my father, who made trips in his small truck from the Toy Shop to many points in town, as did a sizable corps of fathers late on Christmas Eve.

When World War II thinned the ranks of Boy Scout leaders and other family breadwinners, there was no lessening of the need for the Toy Shop's output. However, it had to fold by the end of the 1930s. Calgary's firemen, who had experienced the annual flood of reparable toys, took over the job from the Toy Shop and were worthy successors. ✳

from *Days Gone By: Jack Peach on Calgary's Past*—fond memories of the city

The Sleigh-Bells* BY SUSANNA MOODIE

ONTARIO 1850s

'Tis merry to hear, at the evening time,
By the blazing hearth the sleigh-bells' chime;
To know the bounding steeds bring near
The loved one to our bosom dear.
Ah, lightly we spring the fire to raise,
Till the rafters glow with the ruddy blaze;
Those merry sleigh-bells, our hearts keep time
Responsive to their fairy chime.
Ding-dong, ding-dong, o'er vale and hill,
Their welcome notes are trembling still.

'Tis he, and blithely the gay bells sound,
As his sleigh glides over the frozen ground;
Hark! he has pass'd the dark pine wood,
He crosses now the ice-bound flood,
And hails the light at the open door
That tells his toilsome journey's o'er.
The merry sleigh-bells! My fond heart swells
And throbs to hear the welcome bells;
Ding-dong, ding-dong, o'er ice and snow,
A voice of gladness, on they go.

Our hut is small, and rude our cheer,
But love has spread the banquet here;

111

And childhood springs to be caress'd
By our beloved and welcome guest.
With a smiling brow his tale he tells,
The urchins ring the merry sleigh-bells;
The merry sleigh-bells, with shout and song
They drag the noisy string along;
Ding-dong, ding-dong, the father's come,
The gay bells ring his welcome home.

From the cedar swamp the gaunt wolves howl,
From the oak loud whoops the felon owl;
The snow-storm sweeps in thunder past,
The forest creaks beneath the blast;
No more I list, with boding fear,
The sleigh-bells' distant chime to hear
The merry sleigh-bells with soothing power
Shed gladness on the evening hour.
Ding-dong, ding-dong, what rapture swells
The music of those joyous bells!

* Many versions of this song exist, and it has been set to music in the US. I give here the original copy, written whilst leaning on the open door of my shanty and watching for my husband's return. ❄

from *Roughing It in the Bush*

Susanna Moodie and Catherine Parr Traill are two of Canada's best-known 19th-century writers. Born in England less than two years apart, the sisters were well-known writers before they married and emigrated to Canada with their husbands in 1832. They chronicled their experiences as pioneers in rural Ontario, Susanna in *Roughing It in the Bush* (1852) and Catherine in *The Backwoods of Canada* (1836). They remained in Canada until their deaths—Susanna's in 1885 and Catherine's in 1899.

Cold Comfort BY GEORGE HEAD

SAINT JOHN, NEW BRUNSWICK 1829

*D*ecember 22d.—I was aroused before daylight by the intelligence of the wind having changed; it was some time, notwithstanding, before the packet heaved anchor, and it was nearly noon before we set sail with a fine breeze out of the bay. The wind was fair, but we were opposed by a violent head current, which caused a short chopping sea. The day was foggy, so that we could just distinguish Partridge Island as we passed it, which is about a couple of miles from St. John's: a fort and lighthouse are built upon it. In about six hours from the time of leaving Digby, our little sloop (one of thirty-six tons) cast anchor in the harbour of St. John's. On landing, the difference of climate between the latter place and Digby was very perceptible. In the first place, full half a foot more snow lay on the ground, and the inhabitants themselves estimate a fortnight's difference in the season. The town is a good deal smaller than Halifax; and the extreme width of the streets, and the irregular form of the houses, give it a very unfinished appearance. As there was no choice of inns, I went to an hotel of the same description with that in Halifax, and kept by an old widow, who received me with looks as cold as the climate she lived in—not interesting herself in the least about me, or caring at all whence I had come or whither I was going. It seemed to be with her, as with many others of her description in the country (if one were to judge by their looks on arriving at their houses), entirely a matter of caprice whether one was to be admitted or not. She gave me the worst bedroom she had, and dreadfully cold it was.

Different people, at the stated hours of eating, were in the habit of assembling themselves from various parts of the town. One or two chewed tobacco; all spit on the carpet; and there was one big man, who, I was told, was a lieut.-colonel of the ——— militia. He had a way of eating which I shall never forget. Closing his teeth upon his knife, he drew it through his mouth, so as to threaten its enlargement up to his ear; it was pretty wide as it was, and as he filled it as full as it would hold, a sympathetic jerk of his goggle eyes marked always, by their involuntary vibration, the precise moment when each large morsel padded down his throat. After tea, a great basin of hot water was brought to the hostess, in which she washed the teacups and saucers; and then, having deposited her china in a cupboard, she left me and the rest of the gentlemen by ourselves for the evening. The frost set in at night with great severity, and I found the house miserably cold.

Dec. 23d to 25th.—Sorely against my will I sojourned these three days at Mrs. ———'s. Neither entertained nor instructed by my companions, I was most anxious to get away at the expense of cold, solitude, or any other inconvenience. Fortunately, most of the party attended only at their meals, and, having daily business to occupy them in their shops (or stores, as they call them), they came in with the first dish and disappeared as soon as the cloth was removed, being obliged, in fact, to eat against time. Indeed, they used admirable despatch, and by blowing into their soup, and picking bones with their fingers, they contrived to make a very short business, at the same time devouring full as much as they paid for. ❄

from *Forest Scenes and Incidents in the Wilds of North America*

British-born George Head kept this diary on his three-month winter journey from Halifax to Lake Huron, a distance of some 1,200 miles.

The Errors of Santa Claus BY STEPHEN LEACOCK

Courtesy of the Fairmont Banff Spring Hotel

*I*t was Christmas Eve.

The Browns, who lived in the adjoining house, had been dining with the Joneses.

Brown and Jones were sitting over wine and walnuts at the table. The others had gone upstairs.

"What are you giving to your boy for Christmas?" asked Brown.

"A train," said Jones, "new kind of thing—automatic."

"Let's have a look at it," said Brown.

Jones fetched a parcel from the sideboard and began unwrapping it.

"Ingenious thing, isn't it?" he said. "Goes on its own rails. Queer how kids love to play with trains, isn't it?"

"Yes," assented Brown, "how are the rails fixed?"

"Wait, I'll show you," said Jones, "just help me to shove these dinner things aside and roll back the cloth. There! See! You lay the rails like that and fasten them at the end, so—"

"Oh, yes, I catch on, makes a grade, doesn't it? Just the thing to amuse a child, isn't it? I got Willie a toy aeroplane."

"I know, they're great. I got Edwin one on his birthday. But I thought I'd get him a train this time. I told him Santa Claus was going to bring him something altogether new this time. Edwin, of course, believes in Santa Claus absolutely. Say, look at this locomotive, would you? It has a spring coiled up inside the fire box."

"Wind her up," said Brown with great interest, "let's see her go."

"All right," said Jones, "just pile up two or three plates or something to lean the end of the rails on. There, notice the way it buzzes before it starts. Isn't that a great thing for a kid, eh?"

"Yes," said Brown, "and say! See this little spring to pull the whistle. By God, it toots, eh? Just like real!"

"Now then, Brown," Jones went on, "you hitch on those cars and I'll start her. I'll be engineer, eh!"

Half an hour later, Brown and Jones were still playing trains on the dining-room table.

But their wives upstairs in the drawing room hardly noticed their absence. They were too much interested.

"Oh, I think it's perfectly sweet," said Mrs. Brown, "just the loveliest doll I've seen in years. I must get one like it for Ulvina. Won't Clarisse be perfectly enchanted?"

"Yes," answered Mrs. Jones, "and then she'll have all the fun of arranging the dresses. Children love that so much. Look! There are three little dresses with the doll, aren't they cute? All cut out and ready to stitch together."

"Oh, how perfectly lovely," exclaimed Mrs. Brown, "I think the mauve one would suit the doll best—don't you?—with such golden hair—only don't you think it would make it much nicer to turn back the collar, so, and put a little band—so?"

"What a good idea!" said Mrs. Jones, "do let's try it. Just wait, I'll get a needle in a minute. I'll tell Clarisse that Santa Claus sewed it himself. The child believes in Santa Claus absolutely."

And half an hour later Mrs. Jones and Mrs. Brown were so busy stitching dolls' clothes that they could not hear the roaring of the little train up and down the dining table, and had no idea what the four children were doing.

Nor did the children miss their mothers.

"Dandy, aren't they?" Edwin Jones was saying to little Willie Brown, as they sat in Edwin's bedroom. "A hundred in a box, with cork tips, and see, an amber mouthpiece that fits into a little case at the side. Good present for dad, eh?"

"Fine!" said Willie, appreciatively. "I'm giving father cigars."

"I know. I thought of cigars, too. Men always like cigars and cigarettes. You can't go wrong on them. Say, would you like to try one or two of these cigarettes? We can take them from the bottom. You'll like them, they're Russian—away ahead of Egyptian."

"Thanks," answered Willie. "I'd like one immensely. I only started smoking last spring—on my twelfth birthday. I think a feller's a fool to begin smoking cigarettes too soon, don't you? It stunts him. I waited till I was twelve."

"Me too," said Edwin, as they lighted their cigarettes. "In fact, I wouldn't buy them now if it weren't for dad. I simply had to give him something from Santa Claus. He believes in Santa Claus absolutely, you know."

And while this was going on, Clarisse was showing little Ulvina the absolutely lovely little bridge set that she got for her mother.

"Aren't these markers perfectly charming?" said Ulvina, "and don't you love this little Dutch design—or is it Flemish, darling?"

"Dutch," said Clarisse, "isn't it quaint? And aren't these the dearest little things—for putting the money in when you play. I needn't have got them with it—they'd have sold the rest separately—but I think it's too utterly slow playing without money, don't you?"

"Oh, abominable," shuddered Ulvina, "but your mamma never plays for money, does she?"

"Mamma! Oh, gracious, no. Mamma's far too slow for that. But I shall tell her that Santa Claus insisted on putting in the little money boxes."

"I suppose she believes in Santa Claus, just as my Mamma does."

"Oh, absolutely," said Clarisse, and added, "What if we play a little game! With a double dummy, the French way, or Norwegian Skat, if you like. That only needs two."

"All right," agreed Ulvina, and in a few minutes they were deep in a game of cards with a little pile of pocket money beside them.

About half an hour later, all the members of the two families were down again in the drawing room. But of course nobody said anything about the presents. In any case they were all too busy looking at the beautiful big Bible, with maps in it, that the Joneses had bought to give to Grandfather. They all agreed that, with the help of it, Grandfather could hunt up any place in Palestine in a moment, day or night.

But upstairs, away upstairs in a sitting room of his own, Grandfather Jones was looking with an affectionate eye at the presents that stood beside him. There was a beautiful whiskey decanter, with silver filigree outside (and whiskey inside) for Jones, and for the little boy a big nickel-plated Jew's harp.

Later on, far in the night, the person, or the influence, or whatever it is called Santa Claus, took all the presents and placed them in the people's stockings.

And, being blind as he always had been, he gave the wrong things to the wrong people—in fact, he gave them just as indicated above.

But the next day, in the course of Christmas morning, the situation straightened itself out, as it always does.

Indeed, by ten o'clock, Brown and Jones were playing with the train, and Mrs. Brown and Mrs. Jones were making dolls' clothes, and the boys were smoking cigarettes, and Clarisse and Ulvina were playing cards for their pocket money.

And upstairs—away up—Grandfather was drinking whiskey and playing the Jew's harp.

And so Christmas, just as it always does, turned out all right after all. ❄

from *Christmas with Stephen Leacock*

Canada's best-loved humorist, Stephen Leacock was also a professor of political science at McGill University and a prolific writer. He wrote 57 books, the most famous being *Sunshine Sketches of a Little Town*, based on recollections of his boyhood in Orillia, Ontario.

Next Year Country BY JUDY SCHULTZ

S he was a frugal housekeeper, but she intended to splash out just once that year: she was fattening a goose—a big gander—especially for Christmas. There wouldn't be any gifts, and no Christmas tree, but at least she could give them a Christmas dinner. She'd even hoarded an onion for the stuffing, and every now and then, when she went into the root cellar, she'd have a look at that onion, just to be sure it was okay and not rotting or freezing or getting chewed by mice. (She told me about that onion, and one of the uncles remembers it, too, as though it had been some luscious, exotic fruit.)

There were still a lot of eagles around southern Saskatchewan in those days, and it was evidently a large golden eagle that drew a bead on Mamie's Christmas goose, who was strutting around the yard, soaking up the winter sunshine as though he owned the place. Mamie must have been working outside when she heard the goose honking furiously, then squawking in distress, because the uncle who told me the story (he was fourteen at the time it happened) insists that she almost managed to save the bird. "She came around the corner of the house swinging her broom, and if that eagle hadn't let go of the goose she'd have beat it to a pulp, she was that mad."

The eagle retreated under Mamie's fury, but not before it had mortally wounded the gander, ripping a huge gash in the breast. Once again, the prairie had played one of its endless tricks. A clear day, a golden eagle, and it was goodbye goose. For Christmas they had rabbit pot pie eked out with potato and an onion. Mamie was beginning to understand why some people were already calling this prairie "next-year country."

RABBIT POT PIE

Skin out the rabbit and cut in pieces as for frying. Boil with a little salt until meat comes away from the bones. Pick out the bones and put meat in a tin basin with a cup of onion. Season the juice with a little pepper, thicken with browned flour, add a lump of butter. Cover with rich biscuit dough and bake an hour, but do not have too hot an oven for fear of scorching.

BISCUIT DOUGH

Bowl full of milk
About 3 tbsp sour cream
Pinch soda, maybe. Leave awhile on warming oven.
Stir in 1 tbsp soda, 1 tsp salt, flour to knead nicely.

From *Mamie's Children: Three Generations of Prairie Women*—a
chronicle of the life and challenging times of one ordinary prairie
woman, Mamie Elizabeth Harris, 1877–1961

A Barrens Christmas BY EDWARD W. NUFFIELD

*D*ragging the heavily laden sleds over the rough terrain was hard work and it limited their progress to sixteen to eighteen miles (25–30 km) per day. On December 18, they turned up a small creek, a tributary of the Egg River, and crossed the tracks of many caribou. The tracks were not fresh—the herd had passed some days ago—but they found meat, enough for one good meal, discarded by other travellers who had killed more than they could carry.

They left the creek the next day to cross a stretch of the empty Barrens. There was no game. Christmas Day came and still their bellies were empty. Hearne reflected on the delicacies that were being consumed in Europe in this festive season and he could not help wishing he was back in the Old Country. The Indians remained in good spirits. On December 26, fate was kind; they reached the edge of the Barrens at a small cluster of trees and the hunters killed four caribou. The kill was far from where they had halted for the night and could not be brought into camp until the following day. By that time they were so hungry they ate steadily for the remainder of the day. The Indians were certain the worst was behind them and they would soon meet with better hunting. ❄

from *Samuel Hearne: Journey to the Coppermine River 1769–1772*

Hudson's Bay Company asked Hearne to go to the Arctic Ocean by land. Young, tough, and willing, Hearne had worked aboard a company whaling ship and knew about navigation and surveying. In 19 months he walked more than 2,500 miles (4,000 km), from Fort Prince of Wales on Hudson's Bay to the mouth of the Coppermine River in the Arctic.

Malemutes were the dogs of choice for dog teams, but almost any animal—even goats!—was harnessed. From *In to the Yukon* by William Seymour Edwards. Cincinnati: The Robert Clark Co., 1904.

Man's Best Friend BY C.F. HANINGTON

FORT GEORGE, BRITISH COLUMBIA 1874

*W*e found Fort George in charge of Mr. Bovil, a son of the Chief Justice of England. With him is staying Charlie Ogden from Stewart's Lake Post. He, the latter, came down to help us get a fair start, and seems very ready to us in the way of getting dogs, men, &c.

After supper last night we lit our pipes, and we spent the evening discussing the plans to be adopted &c., &c. Ogden is pretty well posted in country. Bovil is just out from England, and consequently very green in these matters. He is a gentleman and a good cook. As his rations in the H.B. Co don't amount to more than 24 lbs dried salmon per week, flour and tea in addition, he won't have much chance to exercise his knowledge of the culinary art. At present he has killed one of his working oxen and we are living well. What he will do for his next year's crop I don't know, but he hates the sight of dried salmon and I hardly wonder at it. I'll put some more to this shortly.

FORT GEORGE, DEC. 26, 1874

Getting ready for Xmas was a novelty. We helped Bovil to make a pudding, and he seems to understand the business perfectly. Christmas day was very cold indeed, but a very pleasant one nevertheless. We dined at 6 p.m., and I enclose a bill of fare, that you may know that we had grub, if other things were wanting.

Soup, clear (*a la Bovil*)

Fish, salmon (dried *a la sauvage*)

Entree, turkey (*a la grouse*)

Piéce de résistance; roast working ox

Vegetables, potatoes

Plum pudding and brandy sauce, pipes, tobacco, and a glass of brandy and water, to absent friends.

Since my last, we have had a few inches of snow, but the weather generally has been fine and very cold.

My dogs are as lively as crickets and are getting as much salmon as they will eat. The trip from Quesnelle galled some shoulders, but they are rapidly getting well under my care. A train dog isn't very loving, but these are very fond of me—at feeding time. ❄

from *From Trail to Rail: Surveys and Gold, 1862 to 1904*—remembrances of life in the BC Interior between 1862 and 1904 as told by the people who were there, searching for gold, constructing the telegraph line and surveying routes for the Canadian Pacific Railway

The First Christmas Tree

Christmas in Nova Scotia
— 1846 —

L.B.Jensen

Courtesy of the Housser family

I n 1816, Mr. William Pryor, a successful merchant, built a house on a large acreage in Halifax. To honour his German-born wife, he named it Coburg House, for Prince Leopold of Saxe-Coburg. To this house, in 1846, Mr. Pryor brought an evergreen tree for his wife to decorate for the Christmas season, one of Canada's earliest Christmas trees. Coburg House still stands, on Coburg Road, a sturdy, elegant old house that is still a family home.

Nova Scotia is renowned for its wonderful Christmas trees, but Sorel, Quebec, is credited as the site of the first real decorated tree, in 1781. The family of German officer Baron Frederick-Adolphus Riedesel, who was involved in the American Revolution and eventually transferred to Quebec after his release as a prisoner of war, celebrated his freedom by decorating a tree for their Christmas festivities. Prince Albert, Queen Victoria's German-born consort, introduced the tradition of the Christmas tree to Britain in the middle of the next century. ❋

Personal communication with Mrs. Justine Housser and her family, who lived in Coburg House until recently

A Christmas Kiss BY GWYNETH J. WHILSMITH

SASKATCHEWAN 1930s

O ne particularly bright Christmas morning when the horses' breath made clouds on the frigid air and the sun sparkled on the white hoarfrost hanging like thick ropes on barbed-wire fences and telephone wires, there seemed to be a special kind of gladness covering us all. While the horses' bells chimed crisply as we slid along, I cuddled up close to Mother on the hard seat of the van. Suddenly, she bent over and kissed me on the tip of my small nose and hugged me tightly. This was a wonderful, unexpected show of affection from Mother, and a Christmas present that warmed me to my toes. Strangely enough, although she made a great deal of fuss over us and almost loved us to death when we were babies, she always seemed embarrassed to show us too much affection when we grew older—not that we didn't know that she loved us fiercely.

After a half-hour's ride over snow-covered fields, we arrived at Clendenings', where Earl was waiting with a wide grin to help Dad put the horses in the barn. We stamped into the house, which smelled deliciously of roast turkey, sage dressing, turnips, gravy, and carrot pudding bubbling on the back of the kitchen range. Our faces glowing from the cold as we dropped off our boots and heavy clothes, we called out "Merry Christmas! Merry Christmas!" to a beaming Isabelle, Bubbles, June, and Claude.

Aunt Marion and Uncle Art Cann and our cousin Howard were there too, and shortly fourteen or fifteen or us sat down and devoured the food that loaded the table. In comparison to the elaborate Christmas feasts we have today, I suppose that this Depression dinner was a simple meal. Still, it's the memory of those hard-time Christmas dinners eaten around a long table with my loving family and good friends that remains. To a little child they did more than satisfy a zestful appetite; they fed a sense of well-being and security as well.

Too soon it was time to wrap up in our heavy clothes, walk out on the cold scrunchy snow, pile into the old van, and start the trip home through a dark night. The good thing about it was that we knew we were going to repeat the whole performance at our house in a week's time!

The Christmas spirit seemed to last all through January as we went back and forth visiting the other neighbours. One night we'd drive up to the Strutts' in the old van to enjoy a dinner of roast pork and an evening of table games. The next week they'd be back at our place for baked chicken. While our parents visited, we kids had some wonderful games of Hide and Seek in the upstairs rooms or took turns sliding down the stair banister.

Christmases were simple then. We didn't expect many gifts, so we were never disappointed when we didn't get much. It was the fun, the love, and the good will shared with family and friends that made Christmas special, and truly merry for a child of the Depression. ❄

from *Hear the Pennies Dropping*

This personal account of a family's hardships and blessings on a Saskatchewan farm in the Depression years is told with wisdom, humour, courage, and love.

A True Believer BY NELLIE MCCLUNG

CHATSWORTH, ONTARIO ABOUT 1878

*H*attie and mother talked without knowing I was in the room, and Hattie said they were not going to have a Christmas tree this year, for Zebbie had found out there was no Santa Claus and it was no fun now, when there was no one who believed. These were her very words.

I thought mother would surely contradict her, but she didn't. Then I made up my mind that I would wait right there to see what Lizzie and George and Jack and Hannah would say. I was afraid to ask mother— afraid it was true—I knew she would not withhold the truth, if I asked her . . .

I must have begun my vigil in the forenoon, for it seemed fully two weeks before I saw the four welcome figures turning in at the gate, and snowballing each other as they came down the lane. Little they knew of what awaited them!

I got a hearing with my brother George first, and he cautioned me about speaking to any one else, for her said he knew exactly what to do. He could show me that Hattie was wrong. And he did.

The night before Christmas he took me out, and showed me the hay and oats he had placed in an old water-trough for Santa Claus' reindeers, charged me to look at it, and to observe that the roof leading to the chimney had no tracks. I observed these things. On Christmas morning, I was taken out again for observation, and found the hay and oats gone, and tracks plainly visible on the snowy roof. There were other proofs too, that thrilled me to my heart's core. In my stocking hung beside the fire, were, carefully wrapped in red tissue paper, a dappled gray tin horse, and a blue glass mug, with "Love the Giver," on it in white letters.

I wondered what Hattie would say to this!

That was a glorious Christmas. The whole house was full of surprises. There were paper balls hung at the windows, and spruce boughs glittering with diamonds over the doors, and a new scarf for me, dark brown, "to match my eyes," Elizabeth said. It looked very much like the pale blue one Hannah used to have, and the color made me think of the butternut dye that mother used for carpet rags, but I am glad to record I was too much of a lady to say so. The tin horse, all so nicely dappled, with a red saddle painted on his back, was the high spot of that Christmas and, though he divided in two before the day was over, I set one before the other, and had a team. The smell of the paint on the horse was delicious to me, and still is the real aroma of Christmas—that tin toy smell.

I remember that Christmas, because it was the last year that I was a true believer.

from *Clearing in the West*—childhood memories from a woman who would accomplish remarkable things as an adult, from securing the federal vote for Canadian women to being the first woman appointed to the CBC Board of Governors. A prolific writer, mother of five, and a tireless activist for the poor and underprivileged, Nellie McClung died in Victoria, BC, at the age of 78.

Christmas Orange BY DAVID WEALE

MORELL, PRINCE EDWARD ISLAND

*P*erhaps the greatest difference between Christmas today and Christmas "them times" is that, in "them times," people were poor. Not that there aren't any poor today, but back then everyone was poor—or almost everyone. It wasn't a grinding, end-of-the-rope kind of poverty. Most everyone had food enough to eat and warm clothes to wear. The wood-shed was filled with wood, the cellar with potatoes and carrots, and the pickle barrel with herring and pork. In many ways it was an era of plenty, so you might say that rural Islanders weren't poor, they just didn't have much money.

What strikes me forcibly when I speak to old people is that the scarcity of money made it possible to receive very great pleasure from simple, inexpensive things. I know, for example, that for many children an orange, a simple orange, was a Christmas miracle. It was the perfect golden ball of legend and fairy tale which appeared, as if by magic, on December 25th. In that drab world of gray and brown, it shone mightily like a small sun.

The orange was a kind of incarnation of Christmas itself, the very spir-it and embodiment of the Christmas season. For many Islanders the most vivid, evocative memory of that blessed time is the memory of an orange in the toe of their stocking. One woman from a large family in Morell said that at her home you were fortunate if you received a whole orange for yourself. She recalled some lean years when she received half an orange, and was happy for it.

For children who ate oatmeal porridge for breakfast virtually every day of their lives, and had molasses on bread most days in their school lunch;

for children who looked at fried potatoes almost every evening for supper and considered turnip scrapings a special evening snack; for those children an orange was a marvel, something almost too wonderful and prized to be eaten—an exotic, sensuous wonder.

One woman confessed that she kept her orange for a week after Christmas, kept it in a drawer. Several times a day she would go to her hiding place and take out the orange just to fondle it, and smell it, and to anticipate joyously the pleasure which was to come. Eventually it had to be eaten: deliberately, unhurriedly, ceremoniously, and gratefully. Piece by piece, and finally the peeling—it was all eaten, and it was all good.

But soon it was gone. All that remained was the hope that there would be another Christmas and, if God would be good, another orange. ❄

from *Them Times*—a collection of historical vignettes depicting Prince Edward Island before and soon after World War II

The Prospector's Christmas Grace

BY W. MILTON YORKE

YUKON 1898

Lord bless this day the seekers' host,
And bless all gathered here;
Grant health and strength and prosperous peace
Throughout the coming year.
And shouldst thou call us from the fray,
For orphans still provide,
They mercy show, blaze thou the way
Across the great "Divide."
Hear thou our prayer, oh, God of hosts,
For wife and children dear;
Grant we may pledge our Christmas toasts
With them, another year.
We thank Thee for this Christmas cheer,
Prepared by bounteous hand.
Bless all prospectors, far and near,
In every unknown land. Amen.

from *Tales of the Porcupine Trails*

141

Old Chum and Scrooge BY MARY PEATE

MONTREAL, QUEBEC 1930S

*T*he coming of snow also meant that Christmas was just around the corner, and from the first of December on that was all anybody thought about.

First there was the problem of deciding what to ask for. I pored over the ads in the *Star* every night. So many interesting things were being offered: there were motor boots, that is, black velvet overshoes with black fur down the front, which we kids called pussy boots, and thought so much classier than the buckled galoshes we usually wore. There were Shirley Temple dolls ranging in price from $2.98 for the 13" size to $6.98 for the 22" size—wearing a white dress with red polka dots like the one Shirley wore in "Stand Up and Cheer." Rubber rain-capes and tams were in style then; putt-putt boats were only ten cents, as were Big Little Books. They had celluloid dolls for five cents each so you could get five and have your own quintuplets. They had muffs with zippered pockets in them; Mickey and Minnie Mouse watches for one dollar; Tootsietoy metal doll-house furniture, which included, besides a sofa and two chairs with a plush finish, a metal radio with doors that opened, table lamps and tables. It was almost impossible to make up your mind about what you wanted. And then, of course, you had to do your own Christmas shopping.

My father was no problem to shop for. I bought him the same thing every year—a package of Old Chum pipe tobacco, which cost ten cents, and a package of pipe cleaners, which cost five. Though I gave him the same thing every Christmas, it always seemed to come as a surprise to him.

He would invariably have just run out of tobacco, and, if not for my gift, would have been without a smoke on Christmas Day.

In addition to a tangible gift, every year we girls gave our mothers what our teachers called "a spiritual bouquet"—a card we decorated with flowers telling how many Masses, Holy Communions, Rosaries, church visits and Stations of the Cross we'd offered up for her during the course of the year.

The 5 and 10 was an exciting, bustling place before Christmas, with its red paper bells hanging around the store, and its tinsel-strewn counters.

They always got in a big batch of new Big Little Books for the Christmas trade, and we kids spent hours at the counter reading them. The books told the story of current movies and had stills from the film on each facing page. The slogan on the cover admonished you to "Read the book, see the picture," and, since we couldn't see the picture, being able to read the book helped keep us *au courant* with what was happening on the old silver screen. But while I spent a good deal of time looking around Kresge's, I did my real Christmas shopping at Meyer's—for the personal touch.

Meyer's place was much more than a candy store. For its size, it offered an amazing variety of goods and services. Outside the door was a bench on which were stacked the *Star, Gazette* and *Herald*, as well as a few French dailies, held down by heavy weights. People waiting for streetcars paid for the papers by tossing their pennies down on the stack of papers—a temptation some Depression kids couldn't always resist.

Inside, there was a soda fountain, a wall of magazines, a glass cabinet full of smoking supplies: such things as pipe tobacco, and Guinea Gold, Grads and Turret cigarettes; greeting cards; the one-cent candy case;

beyond that a small lending library; and, in the back of the store, an area of counters on which were arranged low-cost gift items for people with Christmas shopping budgets the like of mine.

A few days before Christmas I presented myself at the store, and told Mr. Meyer I'd come to do my Christmas shopping; that I had seventy cents to spend and six people to buy for. After getting the Old Chum and pipe cleaners purchase out of way, I got down to business.

"I thought I'd give my mother a thimble, Mr. Meyer. I stepped on hers the other day and bent it."

"I have a few in the back with the thread. They're five cents."

"Five cents? I don't want to only spend five cents on my mother when I've spent fifteen cents on my father. I like my mother better, even."

"Maybe you could get some thread to go with the thimble?"

"That's a good idea. How much is the thread?"

"Five cents a spool."

"Okay. I'll get two spools of thread. One white and one blue. That's— thirty cents I spent. Now my brothers. I thought I'd spend ten cents on each of them."

"How about these key rings? They're ten cents each."

"Okay. I'll get two—a red one and a yellow one. Let's see . . . That all comes to fifty cents. Now I have two more gifts to get. One for my sister and one for my aunt."

As I moved down towards the back of the gift counters, something caught my eye.

"Oh look at the lovely salt and pepper set! How much is it?"

"Ten cents."

"Only ten cents? It's beautiful! Oh, I have to get that. I'll give that and the thimble to my mother instead of the thread. How much is this little glass kitten?"

"Ten cents."

"It's cute. I'll get it for my sister. Now let's see, I spent . . ."

"You've got ten cents left, and a present to get for your aunt."

"I wouldn't spend the whole ten cents on *her*. *I hate her.*"

"So why buy her a present?"

"I hafta. She lives with us. My mother would say I had no Christmas spirit if I didn't. I don't know what to get her though. She's sick in bed and she doesn't do much. Can you think of anything?"

"Why don't you give *her* the pepper and salt set? That should show you have the Christmas spirit."

"And not to my mother?"

"Your mother would be using it when she put it on the tray and took it to your aunt's room."

"But it's *not* my aunt's room. It's *my* room. And *my* bed."

"So what do *I* know from Christmas spirit?" Meyer asked his invisible companion.

After further deliberation, I decided to give the two spools of thread to my aunt.

A soft, fleecy blanket of white covered Montreal on Christmas Eve, heightening the excitement.

Before going to bed, I brought out my pile of six gifts, and asked that they be placed under the tree when it was finished, then, once in bed, I could hear my mother, sister and father folding up the gate-leg table, and setting up the Christmas tree in the entry hall.

After the tree and other Christmas decorations were up, I heard drawers and closets being opened, stuff being brought up from the basement, and sounds of wrapping being done at the dining-room table.

While all this activity was going on, at nine o'clock, Dickens' *A Christmas Carol* came on the radio, and I strained my ears to hear it. That was the first time I had heard the story, and I quaked at the clanking of Marley's ghost, and my eyes grew moist at Scrooge's treatment of Bob Cratchit. No one had ever sounded meaner or stingier than Lionel Barrymore's Scrooge. And when I heard the fate that would befall someone with no Christmas spirit, I was filled with dread. What a relief it was when Scrooge awoke to find he had a second chance!

Before my mother and sister went off to Midnight Mass, they half-awakened me and led me past the tree to the living-room couch, making certain I didn't see anything as I walked through the hall. But after they left the house, I waited until my father was asleep, then jumped out of bed and ran out to the tree. Rummaging through the presents until I found the two I had wrapped for my mother and aunt, I switched the tags on them. When I got back into bed, I felt immeasurably better.

Mr. Meyer, it seemed, had known something about Christmas spirit after all. ❄

from *The Girl in the Red River Coat*

An essential item for the well-dressed schoolgirl growing up in 1930s Montreal was a Red River coat, navy with red trim.

Courtesy of Tourism Victoria

A Victorian Christmas BY EMILY CARR

VICTORIA, BRITISH COLUMBIA 1885

*V*ictoria Christmas weather was always nippy—generally there was
snow. We sewed presents for weeks before Christmas came—kettle
holders, needle books, pen wipers and cross-stitch bookmarks. Just before
Christmas we went out into the woods, cut down a fir tree and brought it
home so alive still that the warm house fooled it into thinking spring had
come, and it breathed delicious live pine smell all over the house. We put fir
and holly behind all the pictures and on the mantlepiece and everywhere.

Plum puddings were dangling from the under the pantry shelf by the
tails of their boiling cloths. A month ago, we had all sat round the break-
fast-room table, stoning raisins while someone read a story aloud.
Everyone had given the pudding a good-luck stir before it went into the
bowls and was tied down and boiled for hours in the copper wash boiler
while spicy smells ran all over the house.

Christmas Eve, Father took us into town to see the shops lit up. Every
lamp post had a fir tree tied to it—not corpsy old trees but fresh cut firs.
Victoria streets were dark; this made the shops look all the brighter.
Windows were decorated with mock snow made of cotton wool and diamond dust. Drygoods shops did not have much that was Christmassy to
display except red flannel and rabbit-fur baby coats and muffs and tippets.
Chemists had immense globes of red, green and blue medicine hanging
from brass chains in their shop windows. I wished some of us could be
sick enough for Dr. Helmcken to prescribe one of the splendid globes for
us. The chemists also showed coloured soap and fancy perfume in bottles.

It was the food shops that Merry Christmassed the hardest. In Mr. Saunders', the grocer's, window was a real Santa Claus grinding coffee. The wheel was bigger than he was. He had a long beard and moved his hands and his head. As the wheel went round the coffee beans went in, got ground, and came out, smell and all. In the window all round Santa were bonbons, cluster raisins, nuts, and candied fruit, besides long walking-sticks made of peppermint candy. Next to this splendid window came Goodacre's horrible butcher shop—everything in it dead and naked. Everybody was examining meat and saying, "Compliments of the Season" to everyone else, Father saying "Fine display, Goodacre, very fine indeed!" We children rushed out and went back to Santa while Father chose his meat.

The shop of old George, the poulterer, was nearly as bad as Goodacre's, only the dead things did not look so dead, nor stare so hard, having shut the grey lids over their eyes to die. As most of them had feathers on, they looked like birds still, whereas the butcher's creatures had been rushed at once from life to meat.

The food shops ended the town, and after that came Johnson Street and Chinatown, which was full of black night. Here we turned back towards James' Bay, ready for bed.

There was a high mantelpiece in the breakfast room. And while we were hanging our stockings from it my sister read:

'Twas the night before Christmas and all through the house
Not a creature was stirring, not even a mouse.'

On the way to bed we could smell our Christmas tree waiting in the dining-room. The room was all dark but we knew that it stood on the floor and touched the ceiling and that it hung heavy with presents, ready for to-morrow. When the lights were lit there would be more of them than any of us children could count. We would all take hands and sing carols round the tree; Bong would come in and look with his mouth open. There was always things on it for him but he would not wait to get his presents. He would run back to his kitchen and we would take them to him there. It seemed as if Bong felt too Chinese to Christmas with us in our Canadian way. ❄

from *The Book of Small*

Celebrated Canadian painter Emily Carr's unique works of forests, native villages and totem poles took her to remote areas of the West Coast. She began writing full-time when her failing health made it impossible for her to continue with her painting trips.

To A
True Friend
on Christmas Day

Special Parcel BY RITA JOE

NEAR TRURO, NOVA SCOTIA ABOUT 1945

The reading room was always kept locked, and it was where the nuns would put the Christmas parcels that came from home. As Christmas approached, new boxes would arrive in the reading room every day. The mail would be delivered and someone would announce, "That's your parcel there. And so-and-so's parcel is there, and so-and-so had two parcels." We would compare: "How big is your parcel? Oh, it's just a little box!"

During each of the four years I was at the school, I looked for a parcel from home. But no parcels came until I was fifteen. I used to voice my feelings to the nun I was working with in the laundry. "Do you have any brothers and sisters?" she asked me once. I told her, "Yeah, I've got a brother in the army in England somewhere. I don't know where he is. And another's in the army, too, and I don't know where my oldest brother is right now, either. My half-brother does not communicate with me at all. And my sister, she had problems, I guess."

Finally, when I was fifteen, I was told, "Rita, there's a parcel there for you."

"Where did it come from?" I asked.

"We don't know, there's no name on it."

I remember I was so happy to receive this parcel, and so anxious to see who it was from. But when I opened it there was no name inside, and I couldn't make out the postmark. It contained fruit and candies, a hand-kerchief, hand lotion and pretty pins for my hair. Oh, I treasured those gifts. They meant so much to me. Of course, after the holidays I told my friend the nun about them. "I got a parcel this year," I said, "and I got all this stuff, but I don't know who gave it to me, there's no name!"

"Oh," she said, "somebody must care for you." She never took credit for the parcel; she wanted me to feel good. I just told her how much I appreciated whoever had given it to me. ✳

from *The Song of Rita Joe*

This autobiography of the celebrated Mi'kmaq poet tells of her early life and the many family problems she overcame before becoming a well-known poet; her works reflect pride in her cultural heritage and her people.

Dining and Dancing BY ROBERT M. BALLANTYNE

YORK FACTORY, RED RIVER SETTLEMENT 1841

Courtesy of Hudson's Bay Company Archives, *Hudson Bay; or, Everyday Life in the Wilds of North America during six years' residence in the territories of the Hon. Hudson's Bay Company* by Robert Ballantyne, HBCA Library FC 3212.2.B3 1875, N7651

Our Christmas dinner was a good one, in a substantial point of view; and a very pleasant one, in a social point of view. We ate it in the winter mess-room; and really (for Hudson Bay) this was quite a snug and highly decorated apartment. True, there was no carpet on the floor, and the chairs were homemade; but then the table was mahogany, and the walls were hung round with several large engravings in bird's-eye maple frames. The stove, too, was brightly polished with black lead, and the painting of the room had been executed with a view to striking dumb those innocent individuals who had spent the greater part of their lives at outposts, and were, consequently, accustomed to domiciles and furniture of the simplest and most unornamental description. On the present grand occasion the mess-room was illuminated by an Argand lamp, and the table covered with a snow-white cloth, whereon reposed a platter containing a beautiful, fat, plump wild-goose, which had a sort of come-eat-me-up-quick-else-I'll-melt expression about it that was painfully delicious. Opposite to this smoked a huge roast of beef, to procure which, one of our most useless draught oxen had been sacrificed. This, with a dozen of white partridges, and a large piece of salt pork, composed our dinner. But the greatest rarities on the board were two large decanters of port wine, and two smaller ones of Madeira. These were flanked by tumblers and glasses; and truly, upon the whole, our dinner made a goodly show.

At the top of the table sat Mr. Graves, indistinctly visible through the steam that arose from the wild-goose before him. On his right and left sat the doctor and the accountant; and down from them sat the skipper, four clerks, and Mr. Wilson, whose honest face beamed with philanthropic smiles at the foot of the table. Loud were the mirth and fun that reigned on this eventful day within the walls of the highly decorated room at York Factory.

But the wildest storm is often succeeded by the greatest calm, and the most hilarious mirth by the most solemn gravity. In the midst of our fun Mr. Grave proposed a toast. Each filled a bumper, and silence reigned around while he raised his glass and said, "Let us drink to absent friends." We each whispered "Absent friends," and set our glasses down in silence, while our minds flew back to the scenes of former days, and we mingled again in spirit with our dear, dear friends at home. How different the mirth of the loved ones there, circling round the winter hearth, from that of the men seated round the Christmas table in the Nor'-West wilderness!

Just as we reached the above climax, the sound of a fiddle struck upon our ears, and reminded us that our guests who had been invited to the ball were ready; so, emptying our glasses, we left the dining-room, and adjourned to the hall.

Here a scene of the oddest description presented itself. The room was lit up by means of a number of tallow candles, stuck in tin sconces round the walls. On benches and chairs sat the Orkneymen and Canadian half-breeds of the establishment, in their Sunday jackets and capotes; while here and there the dark visage of an Indian peered out from among their white ones. They were chatting and talking to each other with great volu-bility, occasionally casting a glance behind them, where at least half a dozen infants stood bolt upright in their tight-laced cradles. On a chair, in a corner near the stove, sat a young, good-looking Indian, with a fiddle of his own making beside him. This was our Paganini; and beside him sat an Indian boy with a kettle-drum, on which he tapped occasionally, as if anxious that the ball should begin.

We each chose partners, the fiddle struck up, and the ball began. Scotch reels were the only dances known by the majority of the guests, so we confined ourselves entirely to them.

Between eleven and twelve o'clock our two tables were put together, and spread with several towels; thus forming a pretty respectable supper-table, which would have been perfect, had not the one part been three inches higher than the other. On it was placed a huge dish of cold venison, and monstrous iron kettle of tea. This, with sugar, bread, and lump of salt butter, completed the entertainment to which the Indians sat down. They enjoyed it very much—at least, so I judged from the rapid manner in which the viands disappeared, and the incessant chattering and giggling kept up at intervals. After all were satisfied, the guests departed in a state of great happiness; particularly the ladies, who tied up the remnants of their supper in their handkerchiefs, and carried them away.

Before concluding the description of our Christmas doings, I may as well mention a circumstance which resulted from the effects of the ball, as it shows in a curious manner the severity of the climate at York Factory. In consequence of the breathing of so many people in so small a room for such a length of time, the walls had become quite damp, and ere the guests departed moisture was trickling down in many places. During the night this moisture was frozen, and on rising the following morning I found, to my astonishment, that Bachelors' Hall was apparently converted into a palace of crystal. The walls and ceiling were thickly coated with beautiful minute crystalline flowers, not sticking flat upon them, but projecting outwards in various directions, thus giving the whole apartment a cheerful, light appearance, quite indescribable. ❄

from *Hudson's Bay, or Every-day Life in the Wilds of North America during Six Years' Residence in the Territories of the Honourable Hudson's Bay Company*

Robert M. Ballantyne, a young Scotsman, joined Hudson's Bay Company in 1841, eager for adventure. He served at York Factory and Fort Garry in the Red River Settlement, now Manitoba.

Christmas Diet BY CLYDE AND MYRLE CAMPBELL

ELMSWORTH, ALBERTA DECEMBER, 1920

My Own Dear Sister Hazel:

This is the third letter I have started and I hope nothing happens so I can finish it and send it off to you. Work had let up a wee bit for "me" now that Clyde is hauling up logs for firewood, but before that I was with him from early morning, leaving the house before sunrise and dragging home the last load of hay by moonlight. Believe me, Hazel, I've found the only way to reduce. Pitch from five to ten tons of green-feed or hay a day and just watch the fat melt away. I helped Clyde build all his fences so far, and those green poplar poles are terribly heavy. This week I just feel as if I'm loafing because I'm not dead tired all the time. It's a two-man job, this ranching, and I'm the other fellow. Clyde and I sodded the roof of our cabin, I up on the roof receiving the "cunning little" squares of sod and placing them together like a picture puzzle. Some game!

Christmas night we are going to have a little entertainment over at Brewer's. Each is bringing something and I'm to bring a cake, some cream for the coffee, and I'll make some fudge. All are to take part in the entertainment and I'm asked to sing something foolish and dress the part. I think I'll put on Clyde's sou'wester, raincoat and rubber boots and sing through some whiskers a song like "Sailing, sailing over the bounding main." The last song you sent is so pretty. Everyone is humming or singing it for miles around. We surely supply the countryside with the latest music. How we do miss a piano right here at home. I'd give most anything if we just had any kind of strings to play on. Isobel and I sometimes get combs and play upon them, but Clyde hies himself away across the quarter at such outbursts, and we don't repeat it very often out of consideration for his musical bones.

Later: We had all been over to Brewer's when we received our Christmas parcels. It was Christmas eve and an entertainment was on. You should have seen me all blacked up and singing "Missouri." Everyone just roared when I said "Hello, Honey!" to one of our shy young bachelors. He almost crawled under the sofa. I surely had lots of fun with them all. I think we are better off up here than we ever were in our lives. Clyde hauled a whole year's supply of ice and is going to build an ice-house next week, and we have just cut two years' supply of wood. Our cellar is full of vegetables and we have all the milk and butter we want.

So bye for this time; we send all our love and kisses.

From your loving sister and daughter,

Myrle. ❄

from *Challenge of the Homestead*

In 1919, Clyde Campbell, a city man from Toledo, Ohio, who had studied pharmacy and was a serious concert pianist, journeyed to the Peace River country and fell in love with the area near Grande Prairie. He and his wife Myrle and their daughter Isabel moved there and wrote letters home full of information about their struggles to develop their land.

Lost in the Mountains on Christmas Day

BY DAVID WILLIAM HIGGINS

YALE, BRITISH COLUMBIA 1858

*W*hen the day before Christmas dawned, the absence of the where-withal for a seasonable dinner was seriously discussed. There was no poultry in town, but at Hedges' wayside house, some four miles up the Little Canyon, it was known that there were a small flock of hens and two geese that had been specially fattened for the festive occasion. It was more in a spirit of adventure than anything else that four of us young fellows—Lambert, Talbot, Nixon, and myself—proposed to tramp over the mountain trail to Hedges' and purchase half-a-dozen of his birds for our tables. We started about two o'clock on the day before Christmas.

The snow, which was about two feet on the townsite, gradually increased in depth as we ascended the trail, until we reached the summit, where the snow was three feet, rendering locomotion exceedingly difficult. It took us till six o'clock to reach Hedges', a trip that was usually made in one and one-half hours. We were completely exhausted when we came in sight of the smoke from the rude chimney, and saw the welcome glare of a light in the window as a beacon for belated travellers.

A great fire of logs blazed on the spacious hearth, emitting a glare and warmth that were especially pleasant to the half-frozen poultry purchasers from Yale. A few drops of oh-be-joyful, followed by a bountiful repast of pork and beans, warmed over for our entertainment, put all in an excellent humor. Although the wind raged without, and the windows rattled, and the snow was piled in great drifts against the building, the scene within was animated and cheerful.

Gathered at the home of Hedges were several miners who had that day come in over the upper Fraser. They reported severe cold and heavy snowfall all along the line of the river. They had experienced great hardships in the walk down from Spuzzum. Several had abandoned their small stocks of provisions that they packed on their backs. In one or two instances, even blankets and cooking utensils had been thrown away in the anxiety of the wayworn and half-dead men to reach a place of shelter.

All these, together with our contingent from Yale, were gathered about the blazing hearth on that Christmas Eve, speculating on the chances of reaching Yale on the morrow. The landlord declared that it would be a physical impossibility for any person to pass up or down the river until the storm had abated, but we Yaleites did not agree with him. We told him that we had promised to return to Yale by noon on Christmas Day with some of his fowls, and that we intended to start in the morning for home.

I had a suspicion that Hedges, in discouraging our leaving, was anxious to retain us as guests until he had milked us of our last coin. He offered to sell five fowls and one goose at $4 a piece. We closed with the offer, and the birds were duly slaughtered and became our property. In the morning the storm still raged. The cold was intense. The building was almost buried in snow which lay three feet on the level at the river brink. This meant four feet on the summit, and enormous drifts everywhere.

In spite of these obstacles we four foolish young men proposed to start for home with the birds after an early breakfast. Several old and experienced miners remonstrated with us, but in vain. We were determined to go. One grey-haired prospector likened us to a lot of silly geese. Another said we ought to be sent to an asylum for idiots to have our heads examined. Another produced a tapeline, and with a solemn expression on his grim face proceeded to measure us.

"What for?" asked one of our party.

"I'm a carpenter out of a job," he said. "I shall begin to make four coffins the moment you pass out of sight, so that when you are brought back stiff and stark, there will be nice, comfortable shells to put you in. Bill here (pointing to his mate) will proceed to dig four graves as soon as the storm is over."

We all laughed heartily, and entreaties were futile. We discarded all advice, shouldered the poultry, and proceeded to pick our way up the mountainside, intending to follow a zig-zag trail. The snow was indeed deep, and as we advanced it grew deeper. We broke our way through several heaps fully six feet high. The wind howled dismally through the trees and underbrush, scooping up as it swept by great armfuls of snow, and piling it in fantastic shapes and drifts on all sides.

Before we were well out of sight of the cabin, the trail had vanished. Every landmark by which, under other circumstances, it might have been regained was gone, too. I looked at my watch. We had started at eight o'clock, and it was now eleven. We had not made, according to my calculation, a mile. Beside, we had no compass and, being off the trail, it was impossible to tell whether we were going north or south. We floundered on through the snow, which grew deeper and deeper as we ascended the mountain. Sometimes one of the party would step into a hole and disappear for a few moments. We would all stop, and, having hauled him out, would press on again in the hope of again recovering the lost trail. The cold grew sharper and the wind fiercer.

There was one fur coat in the party. The wearer of it, young Talbot, who was not at all robust, seemed to feel the cold more keenly than the rest of us. Several times he paused as if unable to go on, but we rallied him and chafed him and coaxed him, until he was glad to proceed. Another hour passed in the senseless effort to overcome the relentless forces of nature. By that time we were four as completely used up and penitent men as ever tried to scale a mountain the midst of a howling snowstorm, with the thermometer standing at zero. Talbot at last sank in a drift, panting for breath and weeping from exhaustion. We dug him out with our hands. He tried to rise, but his strength was spent.

"Boys," he moaned, as he sank down again. "I am done. I can go no further. Leave me here. My furs may keep me warm until we can get help; but, at any rate, save yourselves if you can. I am not afraid to die, but I would rather not die on Christmas Day with my boots on."

"Fiddlesticks!" cried I. "What nonsense to talk of dying. We are all right. Only make another effort and we'll be at the summit. After that it will be all downhill and dead easy."

Talbot shook his head sadly, and continued, "Promise me you won't let me die with my boots on." Tears sprang from his eyes, and froze on his cheeks. He lay helpless and inanimate in the snow.

Lambert and Nixon were strong and sturdy young men and as brave as lions, but they were greatly disheartened at the condition of our wretched companion. Beside, like me, they suffered severely from the cold, which had grown more intense as we proceeded. All wished that we had listened to the people at the inn. But it was too late for regrets—there was only room for action. Something must be done quickly or all would perish. We divested ourselves of our packs, casting the fowls from us if we hoped never to see another goose or chicken as long as we might live. The fowl sank in the new-fallen snow. We saw them no more, and with them disappeared the wherewithal for a grand Christmas dinner which we were taking to our friends at Yale.

While we deliberated as to the best course to pursue, for it was as difficult to retrace our steps as it was to proceed, a sudden shout from Lambert attracted my attention. Pointing to Talbot, he exclaimed, "He has fallen asleep! Wake him up, in God's name, or he'll freeze to death!"

We seized Talbot and stood him on his feet. He was limp and helpless, and fell over again. His eyes were half-closed, and his breathing was so faint that when I put my face against his lips I could scarcely detect the slightest evidence that life still abode in that tired body. We rubbed his face, hands, and ears with snow. Lambert and Nixon called him by name and begged him to speak. We pounded him on the back and stood him up again. Though he began to show faint signs of awakening, he was so far gone that he could not raise foot or finger to help himself.

While this was going on I hurriedly broke a few dead limbs from a pine. Clearing the snow from the roots of an upturned tree, and with the aid of a knife, with which I made some kindling, soon had a small fire burning. To this fire we hurried Talbot.

By dint of rubbing and pounding, and the assistance of a few drops of a cordial commonly known as H.B. Company rum, Talbot shortly revived. He shook off his desire to slumber, but he was very weak, and kept calling for his mother, who was thousands of miles away. The exertion we put forth to restore Talbot had set us aglow. We resolved to keep the fire up and remain under the shelter of the fallen tree until the storm abated.

"By Jove," said Lambert, "why didn't we think of this before? If we had kept those chickens we might have had a rousing Christmas dinner after all. We might have cooked them at this fire."

But it was too late. We searched, but could not find the first feather. So we tightened our belts, consulted our flasks and tobacco pouches, and sat down by the fire. Talbot, having become rested by this time, showed no signs of falling asleep, but he was very weak, and despondent.

About two o'clock the snow ceased to fall. The wind gradually fell from a roaring blast to a gentle zephyr, and then died away altogether. Towards the south, the sky, which for two or three days had presented a hard, steely aspect, seemed to darken. Presently great heavy masses of clouds stole slowly along the eastern horizon, the cold lessened, and the temperature rose rapidly. Then we knew that a Chinook wind had set in, that the back of the cold weather was broken, and that if we could but regain the lost trail we should be saved!

I rose from my place near the fire, and proceeded to reconnoitre. I floundered along for a short distance, but not a vestige of the trail or the tracks we had left in our painful progress was visible. It was now four o'clock in the afternoon. We had been out eight hours, and night was coming on rapidly. I began to fear that we were little nearer our goal then when we started. I saw no other prospects than being obliged to remain where we were all night.

I tightened my belt another hole, and was in the act of retracing my steps, when a sound that fell upon my ears sent a thrill of joy through my tired and aching frame. "Is it the ring of a woodman's axe echoing through the canyon?" I asked myself.

I listened intently, and soon my doubting heart supplied the answer. It was only the beat of a woodpecker's bill on the hollow trunk of a tree. I turned away with a feeling of heartsickness at the prospect of passing the night without food or shelter. My mind was filled with apprehension lest the delicate constitution of Talbot should succumb to the exposure. As I prepared to return to the fire, another and more familiar sound reached me. My heart almost stood still as I paused to listen.

Then there broke full upon my ear the deep bay of a dog! It rolled up from the valley, and reverberated through the rocky depths, disturbing the awful stillness of the forest, and imparting to me hope and confidence at the prospect of a rescue. I drew my revolver from my belt and fired five charges. I listened to the reports as they echoed through the forest and died away in the distance. Then—oh! thrice-welcome sound! Never in all my life did a human voice seem so sweet in my ears as that which I heard utter almost at my feet: "Coo-ee! Coo-ee!"

I must have "Coo-eed-d" in response, because again I heard clear and full and distinct a man's voice, as he shouted: "Where are ye, boys?"

"Here," I cried, "this way."

In another moment a great mastiff broke through an enormous drift and barked loudly as if to encourage us. Talbot rose to his feet in his excitement and tried to call, but his voice died away, and he could not utter a word. He tried again and again, until his vocal cords at last limbered up. He managed to burst the bonds of silence that his excitement had imposed upon him, and emitted a long, resonant: "Coo-ee!—Coo-ee!"

We shouted again and again. Soon from the foot of the mountain there came back the answering call of many voices. The mastiff leaped as if with gratification at having found us, and led the way down the mountain side. We plunged though snow that reached to our armpits, following the dog. In a short time we came in sight of a large cabin with smoke curling from an ample chimney. As we approached a number of men came out to greet us. I paused to look and rubbed my eyes.

"Is this a dream? Where are we, anyway? No, it cannot be. This is not Hedges', surely?" I asked one of the men, as we drew near.

"That's just what it is, sonny," replied the man.

Hedges advanced and offered me his great fat hand. "I didn't expect to see you silly boys alive again," he said. "and I ought to have tied you up before I let you go out in the storm. Come in, anyhow, and have something, and then join us in our Christmas dinner, which is just about ready. You must be hungry."

The "carpenter out of a job" scanned us closely from head to foot, and then said, "Well, I'll be durned. It's just my luck. I'm out $50 on your coffins."

Everyone laughed at this, but few besides ourselves understood how nearly our obstinacy and self-conceit had brought us to the "narrow home."

So we went inside, and accepted the landlord's "something." About five o'clock we sat down to the roast of fowl and goose, and spent a jolly evening. Two days later we reached Yale, where we had been given up for lost.

But the best of the tale remains to be told. It was ascertained by Hedges, who saw where we had made our fire. He reported to our friends in town, much to our annoyance and confusion, that in all our wanderings and flounderings we had never been more than an eighth of a mile from the inn, having walked around in a circle after we lost the trail!

from *Tales of a Pioneer Journalist: From Gold Rush to Government Street in 19th Century Victoria.*

Born in Halifax, newspaperman David Higgins arrived in British Columbia in 1858 and joined the gold rush at Yale before returning to Victoria to work at the *British Colonist.* He founded the *Daily Chronical* and later took over the *Colonist.* Higgins was elected to the provincial legislature in 1886 and enjoyed a successful political career.

WITH BEST WISHES
FOR A
MERRY CHRISTMAS
AND
A HAPPY NEW YEAR

Courtesy of the Addison family

Our Radio City Music Hall BY MARJORIE PRATT

WOOD MOUNTAIN, SASKATCHEWAN 1931

*T*he Christmas concert was our Broadway performance, our Radio City Music Hall, our one-night stand for the year.

About a week before the big night, we arrived at school to see the stage had been erected by the School Board and the green curtains hung in their place. This meant total concentration on the concert and NO SCHOOL WORK. It was an exciting, anxious time.

At home I remember hearing Mama's sewing machine going late into the night long after we were all in bed. She designed and sewed each of us a new dress to wear to the concert every year. Having a new dress on this special night was a ritual.

Preschoolers took part in the concert and were the first on the program. At age five I remember feeling very grown-up standing centre stage in my new Christmas dress with my ringlets in place and wearing stage make-up. I waited until the older boys pulled the curtains for my debut. Then, I stepped forward, curtsied, and recited:

I'm Mama's little darling, I'm Papa's little pet
I know Santa Claus will come to our house 'cause
I'm always good.

Another curtsy and I bounded off the stage to join the other preschoolers in the front row ready to watch my sisters perform.

For years Neen and Vi teased me about that performance, changing the verse to be:

I'm Mama's little darling, I'm Papa's little pet,
My nose is always dirty, and my pants are always wet.

Sixty years later I will admit it rhymes better than the original and perhaps is a truer documentation of my childhood days, but they sure annoyed me when I was little.

Everyone had a part in the concert. Those too shy for a speaking part were part of the musical drills or a character in the Nativity scene. The concert started with everyone on stage singing "O Canada" followed by the opening anthem. The monotones and anyone who could not carry a tune were hidden at the middle of the rows.

Mothers and Fathers sitting on planks for seats watched proudly and anxiously, hoping their offspring would remember the lines of the recitation, a part, or the song they had been rehearsing for weeks. For hours they laughed, clapped, and visited with neighbours between numbers as their kids went through the program.

The last verse of "Silent Night" ended the Nativity scene and everyone piled on the stage for the finale and "God Save The King." Then, all the performers took their seats and waited for the grand finale.

As a child you could feel the excitement, and finally above the noise and laughter in a room full of adults and anxious kids came the familiar greeting "HO, HO, HO." Santa with his bag slung over his back appeared in the doorway and made his way on to the stage. The glorious moment had arrived. The Santa in his red suit that stood before us surely came through our snow-bound winters from the North Pole with his sleigh and reindeer. During those Depression years each child waited for this visit from Santa to receive his stocking of candy, a gift from the School Board, the teacher, and school pals.

This was the only Santa we saw each Christmas. Before leaving he promised to visit our homes on Christmas Eve, and we knew he would. We asked for little and we were amazed at what he brought. There was no yardstick for poverty and so no envy. ❄

from *Recollections of a Homesteader's Daughter*

Five small girls kept their parents busy in this account, by Pratt with her husband Desmond, of her life on their Saskatchewan homestead in the Fir Mountain region during the Depression years.

The Lumberman's Christmas

BY E. PAULINE JOHNSON

ONTARIO 1889

"Well, Carlo, so this here is Chris'mus,
By jingo I almost forgot,
'Taint what you an' me has been used to,
'Afore we come out here to squat.
Seems jist like the rest of the winter,
The same freezin' air, the same snow,
I guess that we can't be mistaken!
This almanac book says it's so.
Well, Carlo, you lazy old beggar,
Right here in the shanty we'll stay
An' celebrate Chris'mas together,
The loggin' will keep for a day.
We'll hang up this bit o' green cedar
Atop our old kerosene light,
It'll make things look somethin' like
Chris'mus,
An' brighten us up a great sight
You're waggin' yer tail, are you, Carlo?
An' puttin' yer head on my knee,
That's one way to say Merry Chris'mus,
An' make believe you're fond o' me;
You scamp, I most think you're not foolin',
I see it right thar in yer eyes,
Don't fail me, old dog, it would kill me,

175

You're all the possession I prize.
Last Chris'mus—you bet I remember—
We weren't in a shanty that day,
In lumberin' tracts with the railroad
Some sixty an' odd mile away.
No, sir, we were home in the village,
With mother, an' Billy, an' Jack,
An' somehow, I feel like this minnit
I kinder jist want to go back.
An' she was thar, too, an' I loved her;
Yes, Carlo, I'll say so to you,
Because you believe that I'm honest
An' them that thinks likewise is few.
You see she had promised to marry
Old Jack, an' my heart kinder broke,
For tryin' to stand by him squar-like
Meant, love-words must never be spoke.
Somehow it got out, an' the neighbors
Said Jack was suspicious o' me;
I carried my heart out too open,
The world as it run by could see.
I stood it until that thar' mornin'
On the Bay, when the storm caught us Squar',
I hope that we both would be drowned,
An' told her my love then and thar'.
Her voice answered strange-like an' broken,

Her lips they was white and compressed,
"Oh, Jamie, I'm glad you have spoken,
For, dear one, I loved you the best."
An' then, with the storm devils ragin'
Far out of my arms she was thrown.
O, God, when I come to my senses,
I was safe on the shore—but alone.
Alone, with her words still a soundin',
Those wild, lovin' words she jist said,
Alone with the terrible sorrow
Of knowin' my darlin' was dead.
Alone, with my brave brother Billy,
Who saved my dishonourable life,
For all say I drowned her a purpose
To keep her from bein' Jack's wife.
I think I'd have borne it quite manly,
But when I looked Jack in the face,
He asked me to give the straight ticket,
I told my love and disgrace;
But never a word did I mention
About them last words that she spoke,
I'd lost him enough, Heaven knows it,
His heart with my own had been broke.
It's hard on me havin' this achin',
This homelessness here in my breast,
But the hardest to bear is the knowin'

That Jack—well—he thinks like the rest.
No, Carlo, we won't be returnin'
To them parts for some time to come,
Tho' knowin' the white-haired old mother
Is waitin' to see us come home;
I guess she looks older this Chris'mus,
An' sadder, mayhap, than I be;
For she an' brave Billy, an' you, sir,
Are all that believes now in me.
Well, Carlo! We'll look up some supper;
By Jingo, the days have growed short—
We've set here for hours jist a-talkin'—
We're two o' the indolent sort.
Well, well, this is Chris'mus, who'd thought it?
The evenin' is goin' to be long,
So we'll have a good smoke an' a fire
An' liven things up with a song. ❄

from *Buckskin and Broadcloth—A Celebration of E. Pauline Johnson—Tekahionwake 1861–1913*

E. Pauline Johnson, daughter of a Mohawk chief and an English gentlewoman, spanned two cultures in a remarkable career as a poet and public lecturer. At a time when women rarely travelled, and certainly not alone, her sold-out performances took her across the country and across the Atlantic several times. A successful author, she is buried in Vancouver's Stanley Park.

The Lumber Shanty BY GEORGE S. THOMPSON

HALIBURTON, ONTARIO 1894

*T*o go back to my first winter in a lumber shanty. I may say I got to like the life very much. The time went by very swiftly; Xmas seemed to come quickly, and on Xmas day I was sorry we had not some of Mrs. Steve's Xmas pudding, for we had no pudding of any description—but we made out a fairly good feast on the front quarter of an old ox that had fallen over a rock and broken one of his legs, and in consequence had to be slaughtered. The beef was rather tough, but we bore no ill will to the ox on that account . . .

I well remember the first Xmas evening I spent in a lumber shanty. Our foreman sat up with the crew and told us fairy and ghost stories. The crew were very superstitious (most French Canadians are), and for that matter I am myself. That Xmas evening there was a fearful gale blowing, and towards midnight, when our foreman was in the middle of one of his blood-curdling and hair-lifting stories, the crew all gathered around him with their eyes fairly bulging out, crash, bang! Down came right amongst us a big pine limb which the wind had broken from a huge pine tree that stood some distance from our shanty; the wind carried the limb and dropped it down our caboose chimney, and it made a fearful crash when it struck our pots and kettles. A more frightened crew I never saw, and I guess we all thought the devil had us. After we recovered a little from our fright, the foreman said it was sent as a warning to someone who was neglecting his religious duties, and he looked straight at me when he said it. I retorted by saying that I thought it had been sent to stop him telling such infernal lies. After a hearty laugh we all retired to our beds for the night. ✳

from *The Life of a Lumberman*

Exactly who George Thompson was is a mystery. He traded identities with a fellow passenger on a voyage from England to Montreal. He hinted at being a member of an important British family, although he lived and worked as a lumberman in Eastern Canada for most of his life.

Carrot Pudding A DOW FAMILY RECIPE

A Merry Christmas

AND

SINCERE WISHES FOR A HAPPY NEW YEAR

Courtesy of the Addison family

*T*his recipe has been tenderly safeguarded by my friend Christine Dow's family for 75 years. It was written on the back of a page from an October, 1930, calendar. In the Dirty Thirties there was no money on her grandparent's farm for expensive ingredients to make a Christmas pudding, and her grandmother, Lottie Trewartha, improvised.

1 cup grated carrots

1 cup grated potatoes

1 cup raisins

2 cups flour

1 cup sugar

1 cup suet

1 cup currants

1 tsp soda

a little spice and salt

Boil 3 hours.

A Notable Year BY DEREK PETHICK

VANCOUVER, BRITISH COLUMBIA 1886

*L*ater in the month, greetings were exchanged by telegraph between New Westminster and "Old Westminster" (i.e. London.) Once this would have taken several months, now less than five minutes; so greatly had communication been revolutionized in but a single generation.

Soon afterwards it was Christmas, and something of the feeling in Vancouver on this occasion may be judged from the fact that the mayor passed the word that minor infractions of the law should be observed with a blind eye, as he "thought the duty of the police force on that day was to ensure that everyone had his share of happiness, rather than bother about making arrests. It was close to our duty that day to find anyone who was moping alone in shack or tent and see he got out and enjoyed himself . . . We did not have much of a jail to put anyone in anyway, and no one would have been cruel enough to chain a man up to a stump just because he had had a drink or two."

And so ran out the last few days in the most remarkable year in the history of the community. Built, destroyed, and now rebuilt again, already it had amply justified the faith which had been placed on it. ❊

from *Vancouver—The Pioneer Years*—stories of momentous events in the history of the fledgling city of Vancouver from 1774 to 1887

Courtesy of the Fairmont Banff Springs Hotel

Doll's Delight BY BESS BURROWS RIVETT

ST. LAMBERT, QUEBEC ABOUT 1928

*T*hat Christmas, Mary had received a beautiful doll from Santa Claus and she was allowed to take this lovely treasure to church.

During those years in St. Lambert, there was a gentleman named Mr. Kerr who used to dress up as Santa Claus each Christmas morning and, with a sack of toys over his shoulder and a bunch of balloons in his hand, would walk up and down the streets adjacent to where he lived. As luck would have it this Christmas morning, as our family was returning from church, who should we meet but Mr. Kerr in his Santa Claus suit, balloons and all.

As fast as her little feet would carry her, Mary flew up to Santa Claus.

"Thank you! Thank you!" she said, holding out her doll for inspection. "She's just exactly what I wanted. How did you know? She's my favourite! Thank you! Thank you!"

Santa was delighted and patted her on the head and gave each child a balloon.

"Merry Christmas! Merry Christmas!" cried Santa, then turned to resume his walk.

"Merry Christmas, Santa," came the chorus, and for many years after, long past the tender age of innocence, Mary and Isabel believed in Santa. And why wouldn't they? They had heard his sleigh bells and seen him for themselves on Christmas morning. ❋

from *Looking Back*—family memories of growing up near Montreal
early in the 20th century

The Parlour Secret BY SARAH FRASER

BALBRAE, NOVA SCOTIA EARLY 1900s

O f my first three Christmases I have no recollection, but the fourth
one probably marks the beginning of conscious memory for me.
For some reason, which I probably never knew, my maternal grandfather
decided to call his clan home for the Yuletide celebration, and we were
duly summoned to festivities. Clothed in our best—in my case a white
"bearskin" coat and hat—we set forth on the short train ride to Mother's
old home. When we reached our destination, we found my youngest uncle
waiting for us with the handsome two-seated sleigh, and the even hand-
somer horses, well blanketed against the December cold. We snuggled
down into the cosy furry robes for the four-mile drive which carried us
past farmsteads of such obvious prosperity that even I was impressed.
When we reached Mother's old home, the door was already opened, and a
whole bevy of plump, buzzing aunties were struggling to be the first to
welcome the travellers. Inside were many wonders—wood-burning fur-
nace in the basement that warmed the entire house, even the upstairs,
white linen "protectors" to cover the stair carpet, which was not a hand-
hooked one, like ours at home, crocheted covers on the bedroom dishes,
and two parlours, back and front. But the thing that I liked best was the
attic, reached by an easy flight of steps, not by a ladder as in the houses I
knew best, well-floored and the storeroom of innumerable old books and
magazines, all neatly arranged in orderly piles. What hours of quiet bliss I
spent among them. Here, I am sure, were copies of the very first order-
house catalogues ever produced in Canada and many copies of a fashion
magazine which must have been Godey's Lady's Book. There were also

187

many trunks and boxes, but my courage was never quite equal to opening these. How I wish I had!

As I made my microscopic progress among the grownups and through the spacious rooms, I was aware of a great deal of happy excitement. The front parlour doors were firmly closed to my timid hand, but every now and then two or three adults disappeared into that mysterious territory, remained for a few moments, and returned with much excited whispering. What could be in there? The great evening came, and we ate the traditional supper of head cheese, plum bread and wild strawberry preserves—fortified of course by other cold meats, various breads, cakes, and doughnuts—and I was hurried away to a feather bed, so deep and warm that wakefulness was impossible.

In the morning, the house was fairly vibrating with an extraordinary activity. Barn chores and breakfast were disposed of in less than no time. Even before the dishes were washed, we all rushed to the back parlour, where one of the aunties was playing Jolly Old Saint Nicholas on the organ. Someone opened the doors between the parlours, and there, occupying about half of the big front room, It stood. Its widespread branches were ornamented with five or six huge tissue paper chains—not in the now traditional red and green, but in pink, pale blue and yellow. Barley sugar animals—popularly known as "Animal" candy—and cheesecloth bags stuffed with toothsome goodies hung from every sturdy twig. Dainty little gold-and silver-colored bells, and strands of tinsel completed this work of art. There were no candles—a wise provision considering the highly inflammable decorations, but the long, gray sticks of sparklers hung here and there, artfully concealed behind the tinsel and ready to provide the final touch of glow at the appropriate moment. All this was wonderful enough for a small girl who had never known a Christmas tree, but all around the lower branches that swept the floor were many parcels, wrapped in white tissue paper and tied with rosy ribbons, and among them a great, big, beautiful doll and a carriage for her to ride in. There was also an enormous bouncing ball, a horn that made an ear-splitting noise, several picture books, a bracelet, and a silver locket with a pearl in its heart-shaped spangle. I cannot recall that I played with any of these, or said a word during the rest of the day—I was in a state of deep shock. I must have been a great disappointment to the generous uncles and aunties who had provided all these presents. ❄

from *Pasture Spruce*—recollections of rural life on an apple farm in Nova Scotia at the turn of the 19th century

Tandem Sleigh Drive. Montreal.

Merry-Go-Round BY ANGUS MACLEAN

SADDLEVILLE, SASKATCHEWAN 1910

O n Christmas Day, nature first threatened me with something more than hardship, and began to fill me with a sense of her beauty and sovereignty that never left me. It was Sunday, and I easily made the trip to Amos and back on my pine boards. At noon, I decided to take advantage of Algy's offer to let me have his horses. He was away and didn't need them. I hitched two of the enormous beasts to a stoneboat on which I fixed a box covered with a horse blanket for a seat. I rode in style to Saddleville, and so rapidly that I was an hour early. I used this hour to visit Mr. Patrick, an old man, who sat at his window day after day and watched the mad life of a new age go about its frantic business without a thought for him. He was as pleased as a child with this, as with many other calls I made on him. I then preached about Three Wise Men at the little school-house, and lightheartedly set out for home again. I stopped at the Coulters, and they gave me an early supper so that I could get back before it was too dark. On leaving, they advised me to "give the horses their heads" if I should by any chance get off the trail; so when darkness came I tied up the lines loosely, lay down on my back on the stoneboat, and started to sing, trusting the horses' sense of direction absolutely.

The earth was like a white ball suspended in a starry vault. My bachelor friend was a student of the heavens, and he had taught me something about constellations. I searched for the ones I could name as I sang. After what seemed like enough time to allow the horses to take me home, I peered into the snow in front of blunt runners. We were following a hard-beaten trail! Further observation convinced me that it was not a highway, for I

191

could see the untrampled prairie wool sticking up here and there where the snow had blown off. I then discovered that the horses had turned in a circle and were following their own trail round and round. Making cautious maneuvers to get my bearings, which was impossible except in a general way, I pulled the team from their merry-go-round and headed them as nearly as I could guess toward home. When I hung up the lines again, the animals immediately began milling around a radius of about two hundred yards. After repeating these manoeuvres several times, I knew I had to take matters into my hands. By this time, I had little certainly of my position and nothing but the stars to guide me to a shack on what looked like an uninhabited, limitless, and unvarying world. Finally, I set the horses' ears against the outstretched arms of Andromeda, thinking that in that direction I might strike the trail from town.

I thought the ride would never end. The largest of the horses, an animal weighing nearly a ton, fell in a slough-hole and wished to stay right there. I had to unhitch them, and while I coaxed one huge creature to his feet the other took a notion to start for parts unknown. I retrieved the deserter, convinced the other than he should try again, and continued the journey toward the chained lady of the heavens. It was a strange experience to be lost on a night when the whole world sang of the Star of Bethlehem, and to be confronted with so many brilliant stars that one was utterly bewildered. I thought, sacrilegiously, "If Jesus had been born in that cussed shack, they never would have found Him!"

I did find the trail to town, but it was at a point four miles farther from my shack than I was when I left Coulters'. Seven and half hours I had spent to no purpose. I visited the Coulters' again, and Billy volunteered to get out of bed and drive me home, which he did with the unerring instinct of a migrating bird. He chuckled to himself over it so that I felt like punching him. At last he had had his opportunity to show me up.

On no other occasion had I known a horse to get foolishly lost. I determined to drive that team again at the first opportunity, and when I did I discovered the reason for their circling. One was much longer in the leg than the other, and faster. As he forged ahead, the other doggedly refused to improve his pace; they described a perfect circle unless a trail was clearly marked. This and the deficiency of intelligence on the part of both horses, I thought, accounted for my mishap. Thereafter I was willing to trust a horse, but not horses. ⁂

from *The Galloping Gospel*—the adventures and misadventures of life on the Prairies from the perspective of an inexperienced young minister

Dirk Tempelman-Kluit photo

Our Field of Trees BY BETTY AND HARVEY KIRCHHOFER

NORTHERN ALBERTA, 1946

C hristmas 1946 was near. We would be spending it at a lumber camp in Northern Alberta.

Our contract was to stay until spring.

We were miles from anywhere to shop, so we would do the best we could.

We wanted a tree, so we took an axe and walked into a swamp area where there were hundreds of little trees.

There were trees all around us, and we could have gotten lost except for our tracks in the deep snow.

Some moments cannot be described—only shared.

The sun shone on the snow, the air was crisp, the beauty of all those trees adorned only with pine cones and snow.

Just us—miles from nowhere—spending our second Christmas as man and wife and expecting our first child in May.

Every year, around Christmas, we talk about that magic feeling of Christmas—the year we had no decorations or gifts, no one came to visit and we had nowhere to go. Still it made a lasting impression on both of us.

This year will be our fifty-eighth Christmas together—with family, friends, gifts, and decorations. But when we share a quiet moment together we think back to the year we had a whole field of real live trees. We will always remember that time.

Merry Christmas to all! ❄

from the *Saskatchewan Senior, 2003*

Older Canadians share their Christmas remembrances in a local newspaper.

Dirk Tempelman-Kluit photo

The Carrillons of the Pine Trees BY GREY OWL

QUEBEC 1920s

I laid out my small purchases, which the kindly storekeeper had suggested that I make, saying as he did so that it must be lonesome in the woods and that he liked to feel that we had Christmas back there too. And being now in a country where Christmas was recognized as a real festival, we decided that we ought to make all the good cheer we could and so forget our troubles for a while.

Personally, I had always been too busy hunting to celebrate that festive Season, beyond submitting to a kind of hypocritical sentimentality that prevented me from taking life on that day; but never being quite sure which day it was, even this observance had fallen into disuse. But I was now a family man, and being, besides, sure of the date, we would keep it in style.

I whittled out some boards of dry cedar, painted them with Indian designs and attached them to the sides and tops of the windows where they looked, if not too closely inspected, like plaques of beadwork. We painted hanging ornaments with tribal emblems and hung them in places where the light fell on them. We laid two rugs of deerskin; these were immediately seized as play-toys by the two Macs, and had to be nailed down when the beavers compromised by pulling handfuls of hair out of them; a pleasing pastime. Having killed a large eagle in my travels, I made a war-bonnet, a brave affair of paint and eagle feathers and imitation beadwork, that sat on a wooden block carved in the semblance of a warrior's face, and painted with the Friendship Sign in case we had a guest. It had quite an imposing effect as it stood on the table, at one end. We distributed coloured candles in prominent places, and hung a Japanese lantern from the rafter. Viewed

197

from the outside, through a window, the interior exhibited a very pleasing appearance, though a little like the abode of some goblin whose tastes were torn between pious and the savage.

On Christmas Eve, all was ready. But there was one thing missing; Anahareo decided that the beavers were to have a Christmas Tree. So while I lit the lantern and arranged the candles so their light fell on the decorations to the best advantage, and put apples and oranges and nuts in dishes on the table, and tended the saddle of deer meat that sizzled alongside of the factory-made Christmas pudding that was boiling on top of the little stove, Anahareo took axe and snowshoes and went out into the starry Christmas night.

She was gone a little longer than I expected, and on looking out I saw her standing in rapt attention, listening. I asked her what she heard.

"Listen." She spoke softly. "Hear the Christmas Bells," and pointed upwards.

I listened. A light breeze had sprung up and was flowing, humming in the pine tops far above; whispering at first then swelling louder in low undulating waves of sound, and sinking to a murmer; ascending to a deep strong wavering note, fading again to a whisper. The Carrillons of the Pine Trees; our Christmas Bells.

Anahareo had got a fine balsam fir, a very picture of a Christmas tree, which she wedged upright in a crevice in the floor poles. On top of it she put a lighted candle, and on the limbs tied candies, and pieces of apple and small delicacies from the table, so they hung there by strings and could be reached.

The beavers viewed these preparations with no particular enthusiasm, but before long, attracted by the odour of the tree, they found the hanging tidbits and sampled them, and soon were busy cutting the strings and pulling them down and eating them with great gusto. And we set our own feast on the table, and as we ate we watched them. They soon consumed all there was on the tree, and as these were replaced the now thoroughly aroused little creatures stood up on their hind legs and grabbed and pulled at their presents, and stole choice morsels from one another, pushing and shoving so that one would sometimes fall and scramble to his feet again as hastily as possible, for fear everything would be gone before he got up, while they screeched and chattered and squealed in their excitement. And we forgot our supper, and laughed and called out to them, and they would run up to us excitedly and back to the tree with little squawks as if to say "Looky! What we found!" And when they could eat no more they commenced to carry away provision against the morrow, sometimes between their teeth, on all fours, or staggering along erect with some prized tidbit, clutched tightly in their arms, each apparently bent on getting all that could be got while it lasted. And when we thought they had enough and no longer made replacements, McGinty, the wise and the thrifty, pulled down the tree and started away with it, as though she figured on another crop appearing later and had decided to corner the source of supply.

It was the best fun of the evening, and instead of us making a festival for them, they made one for us, and provided us with a Christmas entertainment such as had never before been seen in any other home, I'm pretty sure. And Anahareo was so happy to see her tree well appreciated, and the beaver were so happy to patronize it, and everybody seemed to be so thoroughly enjoying themselves, that I perforce must be happy too, just to see them so.

Stuffed to the ears, and having a goodly supply cached beyond the barricade, the revellers, tired now, or perhaps overcome by a pleasant fullness, soon went behind it too. Heavy sighs and mumbles of contentment came up from the hidden chamber beneath the bunk, and soon, surrounded by all the Christmas Cheer they had collected, they fell asleep.

And after they were gone a silence fell upon us and all was quiet. And the stove began to be cold: and the place was suddenly so lonely, and the painted brave looked out so soberly at us from under his feathered bonnet that I put on a rousing, crackling fire, and drew out from its hiding place a bottle of very good red wine that was to have been kept for New Year's.

And we drank a toast to the beavers in their silent house across the lake, and to the friendly muskrats in their little mud hut, and all our birds and beasts, and to McGinnis and McGinty, who now lay snoring in the midst of plenty; and another to the solemn wooden Indian, and yet another to the good Frenchman who had supplied the wine.

And as we pledged each other with a last one, we declared that never was there such a Christmas anywhere in all the Province of Quebec. And certainly there never had been on this before. ❄

from *Pilgrims of the Wild*

Grey Owl, who began life as an Englishman named Archie Belaney, masqueraded as an Indian to promote conservation. He has been variously described as a charming man, an opportunist, a bigamist, a drunk and a hypocrite—and was most probably all of these to one degree or another.

Wedding Journey BY LARRATT WILLIAM SMITH

PERTH, ONTARIO 1845

Friday 26th December, 1845

    Tuesday the 23rd was Our Wedding Day. I rose at 7 a.m. it was 18 degrees below zero & a very fine day. My dear Eliza & I were married by

Parson Harris at 10 o'clock that morning. Eliza's bridesmaids were her sister Caroline and Susan Harris. After the wedding breakfast, I gave Parson Harris 2 pounds, tipped Mrs. Thom's servants 15 shillings, & having rented a sleigh to take us to Kingston, left Perth at $1/_2$ past 12. We reached Beverley at 5 p.m. & after spending the night at Hastwell's Inn, left at 9 a.m. and reached Daley's Hotel at Kingston by 4 p.m. In the evening we called on Mrs. Murney. We left Kingston at $1/_2$ past 7 on Thursday morning in a covered stage sleigh, stormy weather and most bitter cold. After travelling all day & night we changed the sleigh for the stage coach from Bowmanville & reached Toronto at 5 p.m. and went to the Spragge's house where we were most kindly received by Eliza's sister and her husband Godfrey. As I write up my journal this evening by candlelight, I give thanks that we are safely home after our long cold winter journey. ❄

from *Young Mr. Smith in Upper Canada*

Born in England, Larratt William Smith came to Canada in 1833, aged 12. He attended Upper Canada College, studied law and became a successful lawyer. He was appointed vice-chancellor of the University of Toronto in 1873.

Christmas in the Klondike, 1898

BY REV. A.E. HETHERINGTON

Dirk Tempelman-Kluit photo

*B*y request I have undertaken to write a description of the Christmas, which Rev. James Turner and I spent together in the Klondike in the winter of 1898.

The church was opened and dedicated for worship on the 9th of October. On the following day we moved from our tents, in which Bro. Turner had spent seven months, into quarters provided in the rear of the church. These were arranged by suspending from the ceiling the large tent in which the services were formerly held. This served as a curtain, dividing the tabernacle into apartments, in the inner of which the missionaries took up their abode for the winter months. By Christmas a congregation of over two hundred men and seven ladies filled to overflowing the outer apartment.

Of the many hundreds of gold seekers who spent Xmas, '98, in the Klondike away from home for the first time on that day, none looked forward with greater anticipation and yet withal with feelings of sadness, than those who met and took part in church work. These feelings are well described in the following lines, composed by one of our number:

> *Away where the mighty Yukon flows*
> *'Neath the midnight sun and winter snows,*
> *Where the torrent gathers resistless tide*
> *As the snows melt off from the mountain side.*

> *There, a story is writing for future page,*
> *Of a wild mad rush, in a wild mad age,*
> *Of homes foresook, as in days of old,*
> *Of characters lost in the search for gold.*

> *Of a claim down by a mountain stream,*
> *Of shafts deep sunk, of the toiler's dream,*
> *Of a vision blest, in the hush of night,*
> *Of a dear old home, of a fireside bright.*

> *Of a dear old home, in the far away,*
> *Of a father and mother with hair turned gray,*
> *Of a loving wife; of their tear-dimmed eyes,*
> *Of a love that strengthens but never dies.*

Of little ones playing around mother's knee,
Won't papa come home from across the sea,
Of loving hands fondling their sunny hair,
Of a face upturned in a silent prayer.

With such feeling, induced by home memories, we approached the day. There was no light of the sun; weeks before "Old Sol" had failed to appear above the hills to the south. Twilight lasted from 10 a.m. until 3 p.m.

Christmas that year fell on Sunday, a fitting day to indulge in memories of home and friends. For two days previously willing hands put the church through a process of decoration, in an attempt to make it as homelike as possible. By 11 p.m. Christmas Eve the finishing touches were completed.

Snow fell during the night. The temperature ranged from 30 to 40 degrees below zero. About 7 a.m., while we were yet soundly asleep, a fierce knocking at the door aroused us. A young lady, one of the seven, had come to ask Bro. Turner to come as hastily as possible and try to console a heart-broken woman, who had on that Christmas Eve, in that far away, lonely land, lost her husband, Colonel Hunter. Bro. Turner describes the funeral in the following words:

"He had been a colonel in the United States army, and also a Mason of the thirty-second degree. He had joined in the mad rush to the Klondike, in search of gold, and, like thousands of others, was doomed to disappointment. After a brief sickness he passed away, and that Xmas morning we were to take part in the funeral obsequies of the deceased veteran of the war of emancipation. The services were conducted in the small and poorly furnished apartments of the undertaker, a verse or two of a favourite hymn, a few passages from the 15th of 1. Cor., or a prayer and all was over.

Just then the sorrowing widow threw herself across the casket and, no longer able to control her feelings, cried, almost at the top of her voice, "Oh, Colonel, Colonel, will you not speak to me just once. Shall I never hear your voice again." And had at last to be carried away. Then we put the casket, covered with stars and stripes and emblems of the Masonic order, on a sleigh and quietly wound our way to the little burying place overlooking the Klondike River and more than 1,000 feet above the City of Dawson, and laid away in its icy bed all that was mortal.

In Bro. Turner's absence, I conducted the morning service. The text was Mark 1:55, "Is Not This the Carpenter's Son?" The church was filled; the audience gave the best of attention. After the service, about 125 remained for class. In this meeting the climax was reached, when the spirit of God was manifest in great power.

Dr. Rogers of Sault Ste. Marie led. After singing, the saintly Bro. Casper of Seattle led in prayer, in the course of which he asked God to bless his little girl at home, from whom he had just received a letter saying she was ill. This found a sympathetic chord in every heart. Then Mrs. Ed Rogers of Winnipeg sang "The Home Land." Such a flood of home memories rushed into the minds of all that every eye was suffused with tears, and when, after the song, the leader told of how he had received a letter from his little boy, in which he wondered how it was that God had taken his mamma home to heaven and his papa away to the Klondike and left him alone on Christmas. Such a wave of emotion came over the people that no one could say anything for a time but sob. Then, as it were, all were filled with spirit and began to speak—one after another in quick succession. Men who had never taken part in a class meeting spoke in tears. All spoke of home and of the goodness and providential care of God, until the building seemed surcharged with the presence of the Most High.

Some who took part in that Christmas morning class have since gone home. Others are scattered here and there in many lands, and few of us shall ever meet here again; no one shall ever forget it, and when we all meet around the throne, it will be a glad reminiscence to recall.

In the evening Bro. Turner, "a man full of the Holy Ghost and of faith," preached to a packed house. By 10 p.m. all had left for their humble cabins, and before retiring I spent the last hour of the day thinking of the memories the day had recalled and of the first Christmas I spent in Dawson. ❄

from the *Methodist Recorder, December 1906*

Christmas Greetings.

Red and White BY FRED EDGE

*D*avid arrived back home, as he had promised he would, on Christmas Eve. Because it was their first Christmas in their new home, Charlotte wanted it to be special. She knew it could not be like the well-remembered ones in Clinton, with all the shops as gay as giftwrap and the continuous comings and goings at her father's house. Still, she determined to do her best. Fresh eggs, cream, and butter from their own hens and cow had gone into the cookies and shortbreads. Instead of the spiced shoulder of beef, bagged in white linen, that had always been a part of their Christmas, a saddle of venison hung from the ceiling of the root cellar. In place of the usual barrel of fresh oysters, there were steaks cut from sturgeon gaffed in the whitewater at the foot of Whitemouth Falls. Charlotte's father had arrived the day before David did. His contribution, which he had brought with him from back East, was the wheel of a well-aged white Cheddar cheese.

On Christmas Day, Charlotte was busy dividing the dinner chores among herself and her three older daughters when David came into the kitchen. He had a frown on his face. "There is a man at the door," he said, "He has heard that we welcome preachers and asks permission to hold a service."

While he had never actually said as much, Charlotte knew that David did not fully approve of this. He had a strong sense of family privacy and an unshakeable faith as a Presbyterian. "We have opened our doors to Anglicans, Methodists, and Roman Catholics, as well as our own," he said. "Now we have a man of no particular religious stripe, an evangelist, apparently, who calls himself Father Christmas."

"Does he look like Father Christmas?" asked Charlotte. David missed the veiled smile. "Well, I suppose he does," he admitted. "At any rate, he has a white beard and wears a red toque."

"Then what better person to welcome into our home on Christmas Day?" asked Charlotte. She slipped an arm through her husband's. "Do ask Father Christmas if he would care to join us for dinner." ❄

from *The Iron Rose*

In 1870 Charlotte Ross, aged 27 and the mother of three children, left Montreal to attend the Woman's Medical College in Pennsylvania. Canadian medical colleges wouldn't accept women at that time. She returned home in 1875 to become Quebec's first female physician. Later, the family moved to Whitemouth, Manitoba, where Charlotte's husband and father worked on the construction of the Canadian Pacific Railway. Charlotte cared for all members of the community, and although Canadian medical schools were by this time accepting women, she refused to study again for the degree she had already earned.

Winter Clouds BY JULIANA HORATIA EWING

FREDERICTON, NEW BRUNSWICK 1 DECEMBER, 1867

Dirk Tempelman-Kluit photo

My dearest Mother,

"A merry Xmas and a happy New Year" to all of you—We do wish it you with our dear love, and all our hearts. I cannot write much this time, for I am going to make a vigorous effort to finish tomorrow morning, the drawings that I have begun for you. I have had, somehow, so much to do in a small way that I have not got on so fast with them as I wished. The sketch of our drawing room is for *you*—for *the* book. N.B. The carpet really is dark green with narrow yellow stripes, & the screen is covered with pictures. Several of the "dry stores" (i.e. drapers' shops) are having cheap sales—& at one of these I bought the green cloth for our little square table for 1 dollar & 50 cents. = 6/3—a nice black and green thing— & now this table is devoted to the *tea tray*—for which there is as much difficulty in finding a place as ever there was at home. But already the little table begins to get covered up, & had to be "cleared" for tea!! As I came from school today, I met one of the "Express" carts going into "Orr's" (the Fredericton "Mitchell") full of boxes—Mrs. Coster's imagination (she was with me) stretched so far as to make her believe that she caught sight of our name on one of the boxes! I didn't see that, but I have hopes that the Xmas boxes may arrive tomorrow morning. Rex must be at his office till lunch—but he so much desires to have a hand in the unpacking that I mean resolutely to leave them for him, even if they arrive early. The weather has been very good to us! It had been quite mild, & yesterday the ice fairly broke up & away from the banks, & sailed in huge masses past our windows. It was most curious to see a *path* that had been marked by fir branches, to show the best *crossing* place—& which had originally been opposite to the Medley's house move slowly past our windows. Oh! There has been *such* mud! Such *ploughing* through earth saturated with melted snow & rain. Yesterday at noon it was 43 degrees—and now behold the marvellous variations of the climate!—this morning at about 9 it was 2 degrees—that is a difference of 41 degrees in less than 24 hours. Add to this a strong wind blowing, & a bright sun, & you *may* have some faint idea how it felt as we went to Church. It is like swallowing very pleasant-tasted & refreshing *knives.* The mud ridges on the ground have frozen like stone, & it is like walking on rugged rocks. At the same time I think it prefer-able to snow. There is no fear of getting one's feet *wet*. Early this morning—Clare Coster (she is a jolly nice girl of about 12) arrived with a parcel from Mrs. C.—a quilted jacket, & a pair of Clara's knickerbockers on loan, as she thought I ought not to go out today without the latter articles. Was it not good of her? "Clouds" are a great institution. The knitted veils you pull all over yr head, & bring them around yr neck. The cold really is wonderful, & yet it is *splendidly* fine & invigorating, only one cannot do "much" outdoor work. It seems fatiguing. Today has really been cold because of the wind: but they say that generally when the thermometer is very low, there is no wind, & then it is delicious, as it was that lovely day when we were on the ice. Now you see that boxes could not have arrived at a more appropriate moment. I have not felt a longing for my furs until today, but now I *shall* be glad of them!—I bought some gray yarn the other day, & Sarah is going to knit me a pair of stockings, & I am in daily expectation of a *squaw* to take the length of my foot for a pair of moccasins—for I have decided upon *layers* of stock-ings crowned with moccasins as my *snow* feet gear—moccasins being *warm* & the cold *does* nip one's toes! Dearest Mum I must say goodnight. Rex says it is bedtime—& I want to get to my ("that is your"!) drawings in good time tomorrow. ❄

from *Canada Home: Juliana Horatia Ewing's Fredericton Letters, 1867–1869*

This is one of the many charming letters from newly married Juliana Ewing in Fredericton to her family in Yorkshire. Juliana's letters are filled with her impressions of life in the Maritimes city from Confederation until the withdrawal of British Troops in 1869.

Kamloops Conversion ANONYMOUS

*W*e have had delightful Christmastide services in the Churches in the district. We will begin with Kamloops. Here the Church is a miserable log building, an old store with a low, flat roof, four windows, no vestry, a rough, uneven floor. It was really wonderful how the interior of so unpromising a building could be made at all churchlike, but it was so. For some days busy hands and loving hearts had worked unremittingly at decorating the Church, and when the congregation assembled at 11:30 p.m. on Christmas Eve for the first service of the festival, the general feeling was one of astonishment and admiration. The striking feature in the decorations was the erection of a gothic screen across the east end, forming a quasi-chancel. The light wood frame was covered with red and then with sprigs of fir; in four of the arches hung four banners, which have a remarkable history. They are beautiful specimens of old needlework, representing the symbols of the four evangelists, working in gold and red on a blue ground. These banners were sent out to New Zealand some fifty years ago, with the first settlers that went there to form the Canterbury Church of England settlement. The Canterbury Pilgrims they love to be called. The banners were given to Canon Cooper some twenty years ago, and have since been used in decorating Churches in different parts of Australia and New Zealand. Through the openings of the screen there could be seen the altar vested in a richly embroidered white altar cloth, a present from England; at each side of the dossal which reaches to the ceiling and is surmounted by the words "Holy, Holy, Holy," were the texts, "Glory to God in the Highest," "And on earth peace, goodwill." The principal decorations were designed and executed by Mrs. Wentworth Wood, whose energy and untiring labours are beyond all praise. Mrs. Graham, Mrs. Schenck, Miss Innes and Miss E. Roper also gave valuable help, while Mr. McGregor, as his contribution, provided the timber and erected the framework for the screen. For some weeks, the Choir, under the able direction of Mr. Robson, an old Salisbury choirboy, had been practising Tallis' choral service and a number of carols, as it was determined to keep the festival in truly English custom, so bringing us into closer touch with friends at home. Choral services at Evensong were introduced about six weeks since, and the feeling is already being expressed that a musical service is not only more attractive but also more expressive of worship.

The Christmas eve service, at 11:30 p.m., was attended by a congregation of 28 persons, all of whom remained to the midnight celebrations that followed Evensong. There were 14 communicants. Taking into consideration that this was the first service of the kind ever held in Kamloops, and that the usual prejudices were freely expressed by a few, very few, of the class who oppose every improvement in Divine Worship, the result must be considered highly satisfactory, and no doubt next year will see a crowded Church at this solemn service, and every one present animated by an intelligent desire to do honour to the Babe of Bethlehem.

The early Christmas morning was clear and bright, no trace of snow, and it was prophesied by the weather wise that we should have a green, or rather, as it should be in Kamloops, a brown Christmas, but soon after six o'clock old Father Christmas was about, busy covering the ground with a pure carpet of virgin whiteness, and sprinkling the trees with glistening crystals. Everyone felt pleased with the change, and as the time-honoured greeting was given by friend to friend, "Happy Christmas to you," it was generally followed by the observations, "Something like Christmas this," "Glorious Christmas weather," or something to the same effect.

from the *Churchman's Gazette*

The Doll BY SYD CLAY

PRINCE EDWARD ISLAND EARLY 1900S

*T*he old man sat on the stool, his back against the heavy post which formed the end of the horse stalls. The horses behind him on either side snuffled from time to time as they cleaned up what was left of the oats or dipped their noses into the wooden water buckets. The partition creaked as one or the other rubbed against it. The barn was never quite quiet; they were the familiar sounds that he loved and the animals seemed to welcome his presence.

At sixty years of age he knew that his days were finite. His breathing was becoming more difficult. The doctor said that it was not tuberculosis, but suspected that the cause was breathing in so much hay and straw dust in the barn over the years, and that he was doing some research on the condition. Well, it wouldn't make any difference now, and this was where he was content to spend most of his time. Fall had come and gone, the winds had a bite to them and the first snows had arrived.

In his left hand he held a block of seasoned smooth white pine which he was whittling away at with small sharp knives. On one side at his feet was a pile of straw and at the other a half-finished doll's cradle. When anyone approached the barn, he hastily hid the pine block under the straw and picked up the cradle. His daughter Margaret and son-in-law Alec had observed him making the cradle, but otherwise seldom inquired what he was making. He had worked part-time down at the mill and often came home with odd pieces of wood from the scrap pile or picked up an odd-shaped root which he carved into animal figures. Many were in the house as ornaments.

The door latch clicked and he stopped whittling, ready to hide the pine block. "It's me," his wife Mary called out. "Brrrr! That wind goes right to the bone!" She wrestled the door shut. "How is it coming?" When alone, they spoke Gaelic because Malcolm had never seemed able to master English. Sometimes she thought he was just stubborn and other times she felt he understood it better than he let on. She reached under her coat and pulled out a tape measure. "Here. Let me see it. That looks all right. Supper's ready."

· · · · · · · ·

They had both just turned twenty when he heard of the agent who was taking bookings for a ship sailing for Canada. They had known each other all their lives, both were from large families and both were aware of the limited opportunities for a future on the isle, or on the mainland for that matter. He told her of his intentions. "Will ye marry me and come with me, Mary? The ship is going to a place called Prince Edward Island and there's land for little or nothing."

It all seemed a blur: telling their parents, the marriage, and getting the money to the agent. Before they knew it, they were waving goodbye through all the tears as the ship pulled away from the jetty and sailed out of Portree. Six weeks later they stepped ashore in the new land. A year afterwards, Margaret was born, and Roy a year after her. Now, in the first years of the new century, Margaret and her husband Alec had taken over, and Roy had bought the next farm down the road. It hadn't been easy, but he and Mary had never regretted that sudden decision so long ago.

· · · · · · · ·

"Do you think we can afford it, Alec? It's two forty-nine. She never takes her eyes off it." It was the picture of a doll in the Eaton's winter catalogue that Tillie, their four-year-old daughter, had discovered, and Christmas was near and Tillie knew it. She had told Roy's children that she was getting a doll. "Maybe I should have done what Meg MacGilroy says she does. As soon as the catalogue comes, she cuts out the toy pages before the kids see them."

They sent the C.O.D order in a week before Christmas. The catalogue said to allow three days for delivery, and Grandpa told them he'd make a cradle for her doll. The day it was supposed to come began calmly, not a breath of wind, but the sky grew ominously dark and, always a sign of bad weather, the train whistle sounded sharp and clear as it stopped at Williams Corner a mile away to drop off the mail for the post office. By midday a steady fall of snow began, the wind picked up and the temperature plunged. Alec hitched Bessie to the box sleigh and went down only to find that the doll had not come. Over the next two days, the storm raged. It would not be until the day after Boxing Day that the ferry and trains were running again.

· · · · · · ·

"What are we going to tell her? She thinks that Santa is coming down the chimney, storm or no storm," Margaret said as they sat in the kitchen on Christmas Eve. "It's going to be a great disappointment and I don't think the colouring book and crayons will take her mind off it."

Her mother spoke up. "We've got a secret." She turned to her husband. "Go fetch it, Malcolm." He went upstairs and returned carrying the cradle. In it lay a fully-dressed doll.

"We thought we'd make her a doll even before you sent for one," she began. "But then she seemed to have her heart set on the store doll so we decided to hide this one and maybe give it to her for her birthday next summer." She glanced at Malcolm. "Didn't he make a grand job of it? I fixed the bonnet so that it won't come off because I didn't have enough real hair to cover the whole head, just enough to peep out at the sides." She looked a little guiltily at them. "It's her own hair, I snipped a bit off her braids when she was asleep." Tears flowed down Margaret's cheeks as they moved as one and put their arms around each other. "I'll go and check the barn," Alec muttered.

It was afternoon on Christmas Day and Tillie sat in the little rocking chair Grampy had made for her, clutching the doll close to her breast. Now and then she would gently put it into the cradle, then pick it up again, all the while humming a tuneless tune. The order for the Eaton's doll had been cancelled. Tillie never looked at the catalogue again or gave any sign that the doll she held was in any way a disappointment.

The storm had subsided, leaving a lot of digging out to be done in its wake. The stove was throwing a good heat, and what remained of the wild goose dinner and the dishes were still on the table. Heads began to nod as Tillie softly crooned to Katie. ❄

from the *Voice for Island Seniors*

Although the above story is fiction, sometime . . . somewhere, decades ago, I sat in someone's kitchen on the Island and heard of such a happening. You may wonder at the description of Malcolm as an old man of 60. That was about the average lifespan of a man a hundred years ago.

Rocket Racer Sled BY GUS BARRETT

BISHOP'S COVE, NEWFOUNDLAND 1938

I still recall when I was small, on the shore at Bishops Cove,
At Christmas time I cut a pine out back in papa's grove.
I dragged it back to our humble shack for my mom and dad to see,
They praised their son for a job well done, and they praised my Christmas tree.

Well I couldn't wait to decorate and trim that little pine,
And standing there in the frosty air great happiness was mine.
Then that long, long pause for Santa Claus to visit on Christmas Eve.
While I dreamed at night of the gifts I'd like and wondered what he'd leave.

And I thought "not much, just socks and such," and I fought to hold back tears,
To the folks full grown, those times were known as the Great Depression years.
But I had looked in a shopping book, as I lay at night in bed,
It was hopeless yet my heart was set on a Rocket Racer sled.

I woke at dawn that Christmas morn and searched beneath the tree,
But though I took a thorough look, there was little there for me.
I turned apart with heavy heart, from my meagre little toys,
And went outside, my grief to hide, and play with other boys.

Then as I stooped to open up the back porch storage shed,
There on the floor inside the door was my Rocket Racer sled.
Red and sleek with a bed of teak, it surely was a stunner,
With painted stars and handlebars, and shiny iron runners.

This year I'll watch my grandkids search a mountainous pile of gifts,
And I'll laugh for joy with each girl and boy, to see their spirits lift.
But they'll never see such outright glee as their old papa had,
With his first spill down a snow-clad hill on his Rocket Racer sled. ❄

from the *Moccasin Telegraph, Christmas 2004*

The Best Seat in the House BY MORRIS GIBSON

OKOTOKS, ALBERTA 1955

Joy To You
Merry Christmas,
Fun and cheer
For Christmas Day
And the
whole New Year.

From Nephew Lu...

I t was the day before Christmas, 1955.

Among our new friends were the Gants. The Reverend Waverley Gant was then the Anglican vicar of Okotoks. Dorothy, his wife, had confessed to Janet that she was worried about her husband driving to three or four scattered country churches that evening to hold Christmas Eve services. In that weather, she said, the driving would be enough for most people, let alone holding church services. Besides, the vicar's car was a small one with a canvas top, hardly the "right thing" for the "30 below" and snow that he would have to contend with.

Janet quietly suggested to me that I should volunteer my services as chauffeur for the occasion. I was glad to do that and since Waverley indicated that he would be glad to have my company we set off on this ecclesiastical circuit, first to the village of Hartell nearly 30 miles away where the congregation awaited his arrival. I have often enjoyed my visits to beautiful old village churches in England. This was different. The church was a white-painted wooden structure, an unadorned rectangle of a place with a roof on it, standing cold and austere in the snow.

But the small congregation greeted their priest warmly and his Christmas message reflected that warmth. Then back to Black Diamond for another service, and on to Millarville.

The Anglican Church at Millarville is the oldest in Southern Alberta. Built at the end of the last century, and standing in its churchyard with the gravestones of the first settlers clustered round it, it is a picturesque log building.

The vicar had been able to relax between services, and since we were men of about the same age and shared common interests, the journey was not boring. The snowfall was increasing and the road was covered with several inches of the stuff as we approached Millarville. We were late. I had had to drive more slowly than anticipated in order to avoid skidding, and I felt that the waiting congregation might be growing restless.

In order to help my passenger, I decided to deposit him at the church door, and drove into the churchyard. But not very far. The car simply settled into a snowdrift.

"Oh dear!" said Waverley. "I think you've done it this time!"

"Padre," I reassured him, "just you get into that service and leave me to the car. I'll back it onto the road."

From the church came the joyful sounds of Christmas carols lustily sung by, I judged, a pretty fair-sized congregation.

The vicar hurried off to his duties, and cheerfully I set about digging the snow from under the car wheels. That task completed, I backed the car towards the road. It went back easily—for about three feet, then settled into snow that was deeper than ever.

Out I got again with my shovel and repeated the process. This time, when I started the engine, the car slid sideways. I put my foot on the accelerator and put the gears into reverse. The wheels began to spin.

The congregation was quiet now and I got out to inspect the situation. The car was hub-deep in snow. For an instant I forgot my whereabouts and audibly called on the Deity, but not in exactly the kind of tones that vicar would use.

There was an almost miraculous response.

A voice said gently, "Can I help you, doctor?"

I looked over my shoulder. In my hectic efforts to free the car from the snow I had failed to realize that all was silence in the church. No wonder. Most of the males of the congregation, in parkas and fur caps, led by my friend the vicar, had silently left the church and gathered round my car. My address to the Deity had been answered promptly, if rather embarrassingly.

"Sorry about that, Vicar," I mumbled, abashed. "I didn't really mean to take the Lord's name in vain—especially in your own church yard."

"I'm sure He'll forgive you," Mr. Gant cheerfully assured me. "After all, you've done His work tonight. Come on, men, let's get the doctor's car onto the road!"

Suddenly there was a good deal of digging, much pushing and shoving, and within minutes the old Chevy was standing in the roadway and I was invited to join the congregation. If I wasn't given the place of honour, I was given something better—the best seat in the house, right beside the wood stove.

We were an hour late in getting to Okotoks and the midnight service. Not that anybody seemed to notice. The church rafters were resounding with the congregation's singing as we drove up to the church door.

"You don't need to attend this one," said my passenger, thanking me for my help and smiling, "you've got a credit account on church services at the moment."

"Merry Christmas to you and yours." ❄

from *A Doctor in the West*

Doctors Janet and Morris Gibson practised together in Yorkshire, England, before moving in 1955 to Okotoks, Alberta, in the foothills of the Rocky Mountains. It was still very much the "Old West" when the Gibsons arrived, and they saw the Canadian West develop as they continued their work. A primary school in Okotoks is named after Morris Gibson.

December 26th, St. Stephen's Day

BY CHARLOTTE SELINA BOMPAS

FORT NORMAN, NORTHWEST TERRITORIES 1881

*T*he cold has been pretty severe for some time even before Christmas, ranging from twenty to forty below zero, and the little house not very warm either, for it is but a roughly built affair. Then our supplies have been rather below average this year—i.e., no potatoes since September, and the needful provision of meat and fish, etc., rather uncertain; yet for all this, by God's mercy we have never really wanted a meal, and just now we are having a sledge-load of beautiful fish come in, which we enjoy greatly for breakfast and dinner, and we have musk ox or moose meat for supper, with a dish of dumplings of flour and fish roe, which are delicious! Now, do not think because I tell you the state of things that you must wring your hands over them, and pity and make yourself unhappy about me, for indeed you need not do so—all these things are trifles when one gets used to them, and when one's need is real I find God's merciful hand always supplies it in some way or another.

William has fretted himself almost ill for having brought me here this winter, and he has worked so hard to make the house warmer and he has improved it all greatly, mending the outside of the house and padding the inside with moss and paper, making shutters and window curtains himself, breaking old cases to turn into shutters, fixing deer-skins round my bed and old sails overhead to keep out draughts, and after all, and in spite of all, I am very thankful to be here. ❄

from *A Heroine of the North*

Mrs. Bompas came to Canada from England in 1874, joining her husband, Bishop William Bompas, at Fort Simpson. She travelled all over the North with him, and is buried in Carcross, Yukon.

IN ST. GABRIEL STREET.

$\mathcal{A}$ *Love Story* BY GEORGE STEPHEN JONES

QUEBEC CITY, QUEBEC 1845

Tuesday 23 Dec. '45.

Rose at 8. The weather continues very cold. After tea I went to Mr. Tanswell's. Honorine & I passed the evening looking at pictures in the books I gave her, while Mr. & Mrs. Tanswell were reading. I left at 10. I kissed Honorine's hand two or three times in the passage.

$^1/_2$ past 11, time for bed.

Wednesday 24 Dec. '45.

Rose at 8. Reached the office at 9. I did not go to Mr. Tanswell's this evening. Consequently I did not see Lovely Honorine, and I passed a very lonesome evening.

Midnight, time for bed.

Thursday 25 Dec. '45.

This is Christmas day. I went to Church this morning. I stopped in my room all the afternoon and wrote a long letter to Honorine.

I did not go to Mr. Tanswell's today. They have company there this evening. I have not seen Lovely Honorine since last Tuesday, methinks it is a long time since I saw her lovely face. I am very lonesome & I long to see her.

$^1/_2$ past 10, going to bed.

Friday 26 Dec. '45.

Rose at $^1/_2$ past 8. Fine mild weather. Honorine came here after dinner. While we were talking their girl came here and told Honorine that Mrs. Tanswell wanted to see her. Honorine & my sisters had intended going to see Mrs. Solomon when the above message came. I accompanied Honorine home. She told me Gingras had passed the evening there yesterday. When we arrived in Dauphin street we saw Gingras' horse & Carriole at Mr. Tanswell's door. Honorine said she expected she would be obliged to drive out with Gingras. She told me to go this evening. After tea I went there with my sisters. Mr. & Mrs. Lemieux were there. I gave Honorine the letter I wrote yesterday. We left at 10. Gingras took Honorine out this afternoon.

$1/_2$ past 11, time for bed. ❄

from *A Love Story from Nineteenth Century Quebec*—the story of the romance of George Jones and Honorine Tanswell, two Quebec City young people who fell in love in the fall of 1845. The diary traces the progress of their love, despite opposition from Honorine's parents.

Shop Day and Sugar Beer

BY GEORGE SIMPSON MCTAVISH

YORK FACTORY, MANITOBA 1880

$\mathcal{P}$ receding the regular Christmas ceremonies and festivities there was the bustle of preparation, chief among them being "Shop Day." For the purpose of economizing time and labour, and in accordance with the Company's system of conserving the officers' and men's wages, there were only two shop days practically in the year, the principal one before Christmas, when some of the newest goods could be had, with such little luxuries as confections or sweets in very simple form, a few raisins and currants to give the cannon-ball grease-pudding a semblance to its civilized plum brother of happy memory. Much deliberation took place among all classes in regard to purchases, especially men with wives and children, the process of cutting out articles approaching the fine art from experience. Unlike civilized barbarians, we kept within the limits of our purses, schooled our roaming inclinations to actual necessities, only relaxing Spartan discipline when Christmas, that glad time of the year, warranted an exhibition of somewhat pathetic extravagance in its very poverty of selection. Yet, from these limited resources and opportunities, more genuine pleasure was derived and seen than could be thought possible by anyone who had not witnessed wholesome enjoyment and happiness in the school of experience, where many possessions are certainly not burdensome. With everybody supplied according to the extent of their resources, and the limitations of luxuries, the arrival of Father Christmas was looked forward to with satisfaction.

Following the practical transfer of its charter rights of Rupert's Land by the Company in 1869, and owing to the rapidly increasing facilities of transportation in the development of Red River, Manitoba was created a Province in 1870, and old Fort Garry with its name changed to Winnipeg became the provincial capital, marking a momentous change and epoch in the history of the Company, the head office work and surplus supplies were necessarily moved to Winnipeg, and the decadence or diminution of historic York Factory begun by the side-tracking process of Father Time.

When the reserve liquor was forwarded, a certain amount was kept at the Factory, a foreseeing precaution when the Territorial Government assumed control of liquor, and it was from this source the officers received their Christmas remembrance of old customs, one bottle each of old brandy, port and sherry wine being deposited in the several rooms by Mr. Fortescue's orders on Christmas Eve. During his tenure of office, till he left in 1884, he was able to continue this welcome spirit offering of goodwill, being generous and of good understanding, but his successor, after allowing the two senior clerks—Cowie and myself—the blessed privilege for another year, finally ceased the ancient and much appreciated custom, keeping the liquor to himself. Liquors could only be obtained by permit through the Lieutenant-Governor of Keewatin, hence the well-husbanded reserve at York Factory was valued accordingly, apart from its unrivalled quality. Hudson's Bay blankets and Hudson's Bay liquors are still synonyms of that quality.

The sugar beer was a local product, the ingredients being brown sugar, hops (privately imported), and yeast. The brewing was started in September, or as soon as the supply of sugar could be obtained after the ship's arrival, so as to be ready for the Christmas treating. Watching the process of fermentation, skimming the workings or froth, etc., made anticipation of the finished product a constant joy, and fund of conversation as to its final merits. Not that we could make it deadly intoxicating, but if we could clarify it, by straining and settling, make it show a head, and taste the hops, imagination could do the rest, raising the concoction to the dignity of Bass's best. No one ever got drunk on sugar beer, and good liquor was too scarce and valuable in emergencies to be abused.

There were no "mornings after" in Hudson Bay, at the time of which I wrote, though in former days, up to 1870, there was more or less rum rationed out to the men, to bring out any old animosities among the fighters with chips on their shoulders, who desired to start the year with black eyes and a salved conscience. Many were the stories told me by old William Gibeault of the Homeric Christmas combats, inspired by demon rum in the olden days, when would-be gladiators went outside their houses or tents, flapped their arms, and issued a challenge to all and sundry by cock-crow.

Bishop John Harden, who had arrived in the late fall by canoe, September 19th, 1879, paying his first visit to this part of his immense diocese, had been engaged since his advent in teaching the Rev. George S. Winter the Cree language and instructing him generally in his new sphere. Mr. Fortescue and Bishop Horden had been friends and companions at Moose Factory over twenty years ago. On this Christmas Day, the venerated Bishop conducted the Anglican Church services, assisted by the Rev. George S. Winter. The little church was filled with whites and Crees, bringing East and West together. Theirs was no mean part in making the Indians, men, women, and children, happy for one day at least, in their nomadic existence, with gifts from the good folks in England, and a Christmas tree for the juveniles.

After church service and lunch, there might be a dog-driving for diversion, when each officer or man was supposed to drive his Indian or halfbreed washerwoman, as a slight token of appreciation for his valued services, to make her feel proud, so that she would continue the aforesaid valued services on another year's contract. The dogs, with gaily-decorated saddle-cloths, tinkling rows of round metal bells, carefully-attended harness, and the gaily-painted carrioles, carrying their dusky occupants encased in deerskin or buffalo robes, swept through the gates, team after team, making for the frozen river by the bull track (used in Winter as a means to convey water in barrels through the ice holes, and to the Factory), where racing commenced, to the cracking of whips and yells of the drivers. In the crisp cold air, one felt the exhilaration of the ozone, besides the excitement of the occasion, and another variation of the joy of living was experienced. The dogs knew that this outing was no start on a long trip with heavily-loaded sleds to break their hearts and requiring conservation of energy, so were in fine fettle. They bounded with exhilaration till the bells jingled with merriment. Everyone, human or canine, was infected with inflated boisterousness. Black Care had no place in that racing procession over ice and snow, there was no room for trouble or sorrow in the glowing exuberance of Peace and genuine Goodwill. We had the whole world to ourselves, wherein to give utterance to our feelings, and the air was charged with yells, bowwowing and laughter. Verily life was worth living in such an atmosphere of healthy happiness. Scenes of occasion like this, though few and far between, yielded pleasurable recollections, which even advancing old age with its attendant disabilities cannot destroy, but on the contrary help us to realize the compensations of less-favored situations.

As an appetizer for a good dinner, a five or six-mile run, under such circumstances as herein narrated, cannot be equalled or surpassed. Modern cocktails cannot compare with Arctic air and exercise, and when on returning to the fort, we had given the dogs their Christmas dinner to their full content, had an icy-cold tub, a rub down with a rough towel, a change of clean dry underwear, with our best suit, and new fancy silk-wrought moccasins to adorn our outward person, we felt prepared in every way for the great event—the

CHRISTMAS DINNER

The latest fall fresh wild-geese had been preserved in nature's storage for the occasion. There was beaver, young succulent and tender, wood-grouse—pheasants we used to call them—trout caught through the river ice, the best of lake white-fish, fried on this occasion, and browned to a turn, a haunch of fat juicy tender gamey venison, with cranberry jelly, pastry and plum puddings, nuts, raisins, and figs (if you please) for dessert, with the old seasoned port and sherry wines, whose mellowness and strength was hidden beneath a velvet taste. There was the unequalled blended tea of Hyson and Souchong, unadulterated coffee, and cigars and cheroots of exquisite flavor to soothe desire and make repletion heavenly.

Mrs. Fortescue had directed the culinary operations specially, so that Tom Wood, the steward, had not the chance to mar matters by faulty cooking.

As we crossed the seas or land, mentally, in toasting "Absent Friends" and sang "Auld Lange Syne My Dears," we were filled with solids, liquids and sentiment. What better ending than the remembrance conveyed in the following:

"We speak of a Merry Christmas
And many a Happy New Year
But each in his heart is thinking
Of those, who are not here."

Gone are the familiar faces who sat around that Christmas table, as far as I know, but the board is still spread in imagination, and they are ever present. Is it not worth while being able to frame such a picture of unalloyed enjoyment, mental and physical, and look at it daily. I would my pencil could have made it more beautiful, for a Christmas gathering eliminates selfishness, bringing us nearer the perfection of human attributes and aims, than at any other time of our existence. ❋

from *Behind the Palisades—A Story of the Northlands*

Fifteen-year-old George Simpson McTavish left his home in the Orkney Islands and sailed on the *Prince of Wales* for Moose Factory, James Bay, the southern part of Hudson Bay. For more than eleven years he worked for Hudson's Bay Company, recording the daily events of his life.

Christmas Cutter BY GEORGE H. HAM

Another time I was stormbound at Myrtle station on the old C.P.R. line between Toronto and Montreal. I had driven out from Whitby to catch the midnight train, and arrived early at the station and spent quite a little while in gazing at the coal fire and reading Folder A, which combined to make superb scenery and admirable and instructive literature. Then the village folk began to gather—just why they should spend Christmas Eve at a lonely C.P.R. station is beyond me, unless it was to look at the pictures on the wall, and see the trains go by. But they did, and all they talked about was Mr. Perkins' new cutter, which he had brought from Toronto that day. Finally, Mr. Perkins himself arrived and, when questioned a score or so of times, proudly corroborated the satisfying statement that it was the finest cutter purchasable in Toronto, and that it was a real bang-up Jim-dandy. For two solid hours I was regaled with descriptions of that wonderful vehicle, and its superiority over any other cutter that had ever come of the west. It cost—well Mr. Perkins didn't say exactly how much it cost, but the dealer didn't get the better of him, anyway. He admitted that, after a whole lot of haggling as to the price, he was finally asked how much money he had with him, and, when he produced his wad, they said that that was what it would cost him. And then—and then—the train came in and the conductor and the porter wished me a Merry Christmas, and in the recesses of my berth I dreamt that the blessed old cutter was in my stocking, which was hanging up on my left foot. It was a lovely Christmas Eve. ❄

from Reminiscences of a Raconteur Between the '40s and the '20s—
tales of Eastern Canada from a professed storyteller

Queen Mab BY LADY HUNTER

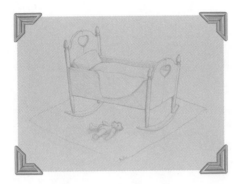

*T*o-morrow is Christmas and the children say, "Oh, mamma, what do you think the fairy will put into our stockings?" Queen Mab is a Dutch fairy that I never was introduced to in England or Scotland, but she is a great favourite of little folks in this and the other Province, and, if they hang up a stocking on Christmas Eve, she always pops something good or pretty into it, unless they are very naughty, and then she puts in a birch rod to whip them. Tell Jean and Matthew I wish I had their little stockings pinned up with the other three, for even little Robert's sock will be suspended at the head of his cradle tonight. ❋

from *The Journal of Gen. Sir Martin Hunter and Some Letters of His Wife, Lady Hunter*

The British-born general was the senior officer of the small, quite isolated village of Fredericton, sent by the British to protect their property against possible threat from the French. He was later promoted and moved to Halifax.

Dress-Up Christmas BY HARVEY BULLOCK-WEBSTER

FORT ST. JAMES, BRITISH COLUMBIA 1870S

T he weather being clear and very cold, and the going good, we did long marches and arrived in style at Fort St. James for Christmas. This arriving at Headquarters is, or was, made a great event. The dogs were made to look their best and the little round bells on their harness polished up with dry snow if we hadn't anything better. The sleighs were most carefully packed, every lashing had to be in exactly the right place and the load properly distributed. Every detail was criticized by the others there to welcome us.

The Indians donned all the finery they had stored away carefully on the journey just for the occasion—dressed buckskin jackets with beautiful bead and porcupine quill-work all over them; buckskin leggings to the thigh, with a broad band of bead-work down the sides, and garters three inches wide of exquisite porcupine quill-work embellished with pompons of wool of all colours. They had, too, neat embroidered moccasins and a skunk-skin cap with a broad band of beads, embroidered mittens, and a big Hudson's Bay scarlet sash.

I tell you they looked beautiful, and were a credit to the squaws who made the clothes and designed everything with the most primitive tools, the sewing being done with an awl and sinews and the quills dyed with their vegetable dyes.

My dress was much the same, except for the orthodox blue stroud leggings to the thigh with scarlet fringe and the white blanket capote or parka (as I think they are called now) with big hood fringed with wolverine, and very gorgeous mittens with fur tops, and, of course, the big red sash, which went twice round your waist, with the fringes hanging down the side. It's a pity that the Indians have lost the art of making these things, and they are very rare now, even in museums. I'm glad I kept mine and many other curios of those days of long ago, and they hang in my hall now—the very snowshoes I did that on and the quill-worked garters and the elaborate bead-worked buckskin bag with fringes, in which we carried our 'backy, pipe, and matches or flint and steel.

It would take many pages to describe all the good times we had during that fortnight—the meeting of pals from distant forts, the good food kept for the occasion, and every native delicacy the North could show, moose nose, cariboo tongue, beaver tail and bear ribs, wild fowl of all sorts and frozen fish of every kind, the white fish and big lake trout. There were dances every night in the big trade room; violins gave the music, the French half-breeds being wonderful players. We did dance and put some life into it—no jazz music in those days, all reels, step dances and jigs. I think the pretty squaws and half-breed girls would have had a shock if we had tried to hold them close and crawl round the room with them a la jazz, and their brothers and lovers would have considered it so indecent to do that sort of thing in public that there would have been knives out and the devil to pay.

We criticized each other's teams of dogs, did some dealing and swapping, and had dog races on the lake and shooting competitions in the woods. We played endless sprees and practical jokes on each other and on the staff of the Fort, who good naturedly put up with it from those young fellows bursting with health and high spirits, who had been leading the hard lonely life at those far Northern Posts for the last six or eight months. ❄

from *Memories of Sport and Travel Fifty Years Ago*

British-born Harvey Bullock-Webster was only in his teens when he decided to join Hudson's Bay Company, drawn by tales of adventure in the Canadian north. He later settled in New Zealand and became the Master of Pakuranga Hounds.

Wily Fox BY WILFRED GRENFELL

LABRADOR, NEWFOUNDLAND 1920S

O utwitting foxes is not so easy as those who talk slightingly of the "lower animals" seem to suppose. One winter, two men from North Newfoundland, who had a plan to get rich by securing rare fox skins, stayed in the North when the fishing fleets were driven South by the close of open water. It came out later that they had obtained from a friend a lot of poison, with which they intended to make their fortunes, though they knew perfectly well that the use of poison in catching fur-bearing animals is strictly forbidden by law.

It so happened that a large whale had been driven ashore that fall; and near the carcass they made their camp, knowing that foxes would be sure to be attracted by the feast. Just before Christmas, a violent storm broke up the standing ice and washed the whale clean away. It took a lot of discussion before they decided to give up the herrings, which they had designed for their own Christmas dinner, to be used as bait; but, as one of them argued, "a good fox is worth more than a meal." So they filled up the herrings with the poison, found a trail on the snow where a fox had been passing to and fro, placed the poisoned bait on it, and hid away to watch results. A fine silver fox soon scented the herring, and, snapping it up, swallowed it in a gulp. They could easily have shot the fox, but decided not to for fear of injuring the pelt with bullet holes. So they watched Reynard make for the woods, and then followed close behind, waiting for him to drop in his tracks. They were not skilled trappers and soon lost their way. On looking around, they were surprised to see the fox following them. They casually dropped another herring and went on without stopping.

Sure enough, Brother Fox gobbled the second herring with as much gusto as he had the first. A third time they repeated the attempt, but again Master Reynard was left licking his chops. By this time he was a bit wary and would not come within gunshot. The day ended with the last herring dropped and the fox farther than ever behind, with a knowing grin on his face. Evidently he was bit puzzled at finding so many fat herrings on that pathway of his. The men swore that he had some internal antidote for their poison. They never laid eyes on him again; but we trust that on Christmas morning he was laughing loudly in his den at the two would-be hunters, thinking of their lost herrings, their lost fox and their lost self-respect. ❄

from *Forty Years for Labrador*

To raise money to support his hospitals, schools and orphanages, Sir Wilfred Grenfell wrote many books about life in Labrador.

Paper Planes BY MARY PEATE

MONTREAL, QUEBEC 1944

Paul von Baich photo

$\mathcal{E}$veryone's favourite bandleader, (Major) Glenn Miller, was reported missing. On December 15th, 1944, a small plane he was in disappeared on a flight from England to Paris during bad weather. He was the

Director of the United States Air Force Band, and was on his way to make arrangements for his band's arrival in Paris a few days later.

Another low point was that it was my brother Choate's first Christmas overseas. It would have been his second Christmas overseas had it not been for his suffering a ruptured appendix in Halifax mere hours before he was to board ship. After he recuperated, he was given embarkation leave in Montreal in August of 1944, then shipped out in September. He phoned his wife from Halifax to say goodbye, then phoned our home to say goodbye to us, but wasn't able to get through because, as my mother and sister never let me forget, I was on the phone, having one of my extended conversations.

That Christmas, who was left of our family: my mother, sister Helena, brother Bill, and I, sat at the dining-room table half-heartedly eating our Christmas dinner. It was no merry Dickensian repast. Without my father, who had always done the carving, my mother had really hacked up the turkey. And without Choate there providing comic relief, the meal was a dreary affair.

Suddenly a memory came back to me, and I said, "Hey, do you remember the Christmas that Choate demonstrated those airplanes in Eaton's basement?"

My mother smiled, remembering. "Of course I do. Wasn't that fun, when he came home?"

The incident had happened during the Depression, when Choate was going to college. During the Christmas break, he managed to get a job, to help out with his tuition. The job was demonstrating paper airplanes in Eaton's basement, but in Toronto, not Montreal. Why they had to import airplane demonstrators from Montreal, when there must have been just as many available in Toronto, remains a mystery. Perhaps it was because he was such a whiz at flying them, and had the gift of gab. He practised in our basement, which had lots of pillars in it, and he could actually, by putting a little English on it, get the plane to go around the pillars and come back to him. The planes sold for 5 cents each. Once he had his flying technique perfected and his spiel down pat, he left for Toronto by train.

He arrived back home on Christmas morning with the most enormous box in tow. (So enormous that he later made me a sit-in doll's house out of it.)

With great ceremony, he opened the cardboard carton, and inside were what seemed to me dozens of presents for every member of the family. He was like a nineteen-year-old Santa, come by train. He handed me three boxes, which turned out to contain Tootsietoy metal dollhouse furniture for a living room, kitchen and bathroom.

"I didn't know which room you'd prefer, so I bought all three, " he explained airily, at my stunned look.

The other gifts he distributed to the rest of the family were met with equal surprise at such largess.

It wasn't until all the presents had been opened and we'd finished eating our Christmas dinner, that he confessed, with some chagrin, what had happened.

After receiving his pay on the afternoon of Christmas Eve, he had felt so full of the Christmas spirit that he went all through Eaton's like a whirlwind, buying gifts left and right, until he discovered he had just enough money for his train fare home. When he finished his story, he spread his hands and said sheepishly, "So here I am, Mammy, right back where I started from." (He called her Mammy because Abner Yokum called his mother Mammy, and he was always quoting Li'l Abner, saying such things as, after a meal, "'Twaren't good, but 'twar fillin'.") But maybe he wasn't quite right back where he had started from. He'd had all the fun of demonstrating the planes, and of shopping, and of spreading all that Christmas cheer at home.

But the best thing about it was that now, on this Christmas of 1944, he had spread that Christmas cheer again. Just remembering that day had brightened us all up enough so that we enjoyed the rest of our Christmas dinner.

Who would have thought that his Christmas spirit would have glowed for such a long time? It seemed that it only had to be rekindled in memory to spread its warmth anew. ❄

from *Girl in a Sloppy Joe Sweater*—wartime remembrances from Eastern Canada

Candles for Christmas

Slip me in
your book,
please do,
I will keep
your place
for you,
And after
Christmas
I will stay
To wish you
gladness
every day.

S ister Lavarty of the Grey Nuns, for some years principal of the
convent at Chipewyan on Lake Athabasca in the far North, tells of the

wonderful recognition of Christmas at that post. A custom of the traders, trappers, half-breeds, Indians, is to make gifts of candles all though the year for Christmas mass.

Several hundreds are thus secured and the Christmas mass is a great festival in the Northland to which the Indians come from as far as one hundred and fifty miles by dog-sleighs.

One can visualize the Christmas scene in that primitive Church of the North, set in miles of snowy mural decorations, the work of the priests and nuns. The charm of twilight dims its outlines, then three hundred candles glow, softly golden, and the magic music is wafted on the Aurora Borealis as it widens over a star-filled plain.

Truly the spirit of Christmas is there! ❄

from the Alberta Folklore and Local History Collection, University of Alberta Libraries

Today a modest, isolated town of 1400, Fort Chipewyan looms large in Canadian history. The oldest European settlement west of Saskatchewan, it was built in 1788 by the North West Company at the urging of Alexander Mackenzie, who then set out from it on his great treks of discovery to the Arctic and Pacific Oceans.

The Surprise BY ADA L. SUDSBURY

SUMMERSIDE, PRINCE EDWARD ISLAND 1928

I grew up in Summerside, P.E.I., in a family which would be classified as poor by today's standards, but I was seldom aware of that fact because most of the families we knew were no better off than we were— and some had far less than we did.

Two annual events of the Christmas season which remain firmly fixed in my memory were the arrival of Santa Claus at TOYLAND in Holman's store and the Sunday School Christmas Concert at the church I attended.

The Santa at TOYLAND was fat and jolly, while the one at our concert was tall and thin. As a small child, I didn't question why there was such a difference between the two; and I joyfully accepted the bag of candy handed out by the Santa at the Sunday School Concert.

I firmly believed that the Santa at TOYLAND had come from the North Pole and that he was the one who filled my stocking on Christmas Eve with an orange, some ribbon candy, barley toys (delicious hard candy sweetened with barley sugar and shaped like animals), and perhaps several little gifts.

There would be a few other presents under the tree—small toys, a picture book and usually a pair of warm mittens which looked remarkably like those knitted by my grandmother.

One year—I believe it was my fifth or sixth Christmas—I received a truly wonderful gift. It was a doll with dark brown curly hair and a beautiful face with "sleepy" eyes; AND she cried "Mamma" when you turned her over!

Years later, I learned that my much-loved doll was a "premium" that had been obtained with wrappers from SURPRISE soap—a brand of "bar" soap commonly used in many households in those days. My mother and my grandmother had saved goodness knows how many wrappers in order to get my doll and a smaller very life-like baby doll for my little sister.

I have received many lovely gifts since then, but I have never forgotten my beautiful SURPRISE doll.

from the *Voice for Island Seniors*

Ada Sudsbury left P.E.I. in 1942 to work briefly in Quebec City, before joining the Women's Division of the R.C.A.F., where she served for three years. She later became a teacher in Quebec and returned to Charlottetown, P.E.I., in 1983.

Gregorys and Groceries BY LADY HUNTER

FREDERICTON, NEW BRUNSWICK 1804

O ur gay season does not commence until after Christmas when the
river gets quite frozen over, and then everybody is flying about in
sleighs in the morning, and going to gregorys and dances in the evening. I
have been at one or two gregorys—stupid card-parties, where you are
crammed with tea, coffee, cakes, and then in an hour or two cold turkey,
ham, and profusion of tarts, pies, and sweetmeats; punch, wine porter,
liqueurs, and all sorts of drink; so you see these parties are no joke.
Besides, in this cold country, people eat so unmercifully. Next week, the
General says, I must begin, but it must be the end of the week, I think, for
it will take Betty two or three days to make all the cakes, jellies, and pas-
tries. I wish you saw the figures we ladies sally forth to these parties, with
over-shoes, great-coats, and immense hoods stuffed three inches thick
with eider-down, out of which not even a nose is allowed to peep. They are
really snug things, and have a deep neck; stuffed too, just like the old-fashioned calash. The people here of all ranks speak good English, except for a
few who have the Yankee tone and twang, which is a horrid, whining way
of talking. Tell my mother she is very good to think of sending us anything
we may want here, but have no wants; all the necessaries, and even many
of what are termed luxuries of life, are cheap and abundant, and our good
king gives us a comfortable house to live in, as much wood as we can burn,
bread, and salt pork, besides twenty pounds of fresh pork and thirty-five
pounds of beef in the week. We have beef all the winter. We have also tea,
rice, salt, butter, and candles. Every part of the ration is excellent, except
the butter, which is so bad we never have been able to make use of it, and

it sells for a very trifle, as this province is famous for good butter. You will wonder what is high-priced. Every article of clothing is six times the price it is in England, and everything imported from England. Good wine is the same price as it is there, without the duty. Servants wages are very high; you can not get a lassie like Susan under £12 a year, and tea, sugar and rum allowed, which will cost £6 more. ❄

from *The Journal of Gen. St. Martin Hunter and Some Letters of His Wife, Lady Hunter*

An English officer, who served in Fredericton and Halifax early in the 19th century, and his wife both kept journals of their time there.

Gourmet Christmas BY KATHLEEN SLOAN-MCINTOSH

NIAGARA, ONTARIO 2000

ICE GROVE.

*T*oday is December 18 and, like the days leading up to it, rather grey, damp and overcast. The only bright bit of outdoor goings-on have to do with the bird feeders and suet ball that hang outside my office window. The chickadees cling to the ball as they peck and swing; looks like a carnival ride for birds. The squirrels hang upside down to nibble at the sunflower seeds in one of the feeders, very dexterous. We had a dusting of

257

snow on December 10, as we trimmed our tree. It could not have been lovelier or better timed. But later that night, the temperature rose slightly and rain washed all snow traces away. Looks like it might be a green Christmas.

This morning I made Ted a birthday fry-up complete with my home-made potato bread, fried tomatoes, mushrooms, eggs, sausages and prosciutto. I got up earlier than him and made a sour-cream coffee cake embedded with McIntosh apples, I don't think he'll need lunch.

We are looking forward to Christmas very much, an early one with Andrew, Ian, and Emma, then Alysa, Jenna, Colsen, Ted, and I. Ben and Chris to be at dinner on *the* day. Am thinking about the usual seafood preparations for Christmas Eve: some clams from Niagara Oyster as well as our favourite sauteed shrimps spiked with chilies and lemon.

As for baking, perhaps a yeast braid for Christmas morning, a Dundee cake for Win and Mac, Ted's parents. Potato bread and the traditional cookies, of course. Alysa and I talked about goose for dinner.

December 24. As if ordered, it snows again, big fat feathery flakes, right on schedule, late at night. We have huge succulent clams from Niagara Oyster paired with garlic and butter tossed with linguine followed by wedges of hot smoked salmon with a lovely Pinot Blanc from Vineyard Estates Winery.

Christmas dinner is prepared mostly by Alysa and Chris. And I have more time to play with Cole—what could be nicer? I make a cauliflower and potato soup, with Chris adding his own little touch, the leftover hot smoked salmon chopped up and crisped in a hot pan then mixed with chopped chives. Lovely garnish with the creamy soup. Alysa took full charge of the goose, stuffed it with fragrant fruity stuffing filled with apples, prunes, and chestnuts. My bay leaf is growing profusely indoors, so we used its leaves to scent and flavour the stuffing, and before our goose was cooked Chris scored it like a ham and brushed it with some of my *nettare d'uva*—Italian grape nectar. This is a dark elixir that I brought back from the Slow Food Festival in Turin, where I had it drizzled on creamy pannacotta. Braised endives, mashed potatoes with black pepper, pickled red cabbage. A true Dickensian feast, complete with dark and light fruit cakes, our holiday cookies, warm mincemeat tarts and wonderful English Stilton. ✳

from *A Year in Niagara: The People and Food of Wine Country*—recipes, along with food and wine-oriented notes, from a noted Ontario writer and cook, who presents her own and local chefs' recipes, using local produce and wine from local wineries

St. Mary's Hospital Christmas Bazaar

BY FRANCES BACKHOUSE

DAWSON, YUKON 1899

*I*n the fall of 1899, when the hospital's finances looked particularly grim, a group of Dawson women came to the rescue with plans for a grand Christmas charity bazaar that was a resounding success.

The gala, a week-long affair, was held at the Palace Grand Theatre. Each day's activities were chronicled in the *Paystreak*, a daily newspaper published for the duration of the bazaar.

The bazaar provided a welcome break in the midst of the darkest, coldest month of the year. People happily paid the price of admission to the brightly lit hall, and then made the rounds of the stalls, spending money freely on an impressive selection of handmade and donated items, lottery tickets, and food.

Although far too busy with hospital duties to help organize the event, the nuns still found time to do their part. Sister Mary Pauline made candies for Mrs. Mahoney's Confection Booth. A new arrival, Sister Mary Jules, roasted turkeys for the Christmas dinner. For the Fancy Work Stall, Sister Mary Joseph trimmed a handkerchief with Brussels lace, and several other sisters made wax-dipped paper flowers.

One of the highlights of the fair was the Turkish Booth, which occupied much of the theatre's upper floor and was "most effectively furnished with low divans, nooks and corners, and the dim tinted lights affected by the Orientals." There, cafe noir and cigars were served by "fair women, bewitching as any Eastern houris." Despite the hint of naughtiness in the *Paystreak's* depiction of the Turkish Booth, there was nothing risque about the bazaar. The ladies' organizing committee was headed by some of the most respectable women in the district, including the wives of Captain Cortlandt Starnes of the North-West Mounted Police and Judge Dugas.

At the end of the week, Mrs. Dugas and Mrs. Starnes presented twelve thousand dollars to a delighted Sister Mary Zephyrin. Although this did not solve all the financial troubles at St. Mary's, it relieved much of the pressure. ❄

from *Women of the Klondike*

St. Mary's Hospital, built in 1898 by Father William Judge, S.J. the "saint of Dawson," was deeply in debt when he died early in 1899. The Sisters of Saint Ann of Saint Joseph's Province took over the hospital and its debts.

Christmas Mummers BY SIR RICHARD BONNYCASTLE

ST. JOHN'S, NEWFOUNDLAND 1842

A t St. John's, on St. Stephen's day, little boys go about from door to door, with a green bush from the spruce trees, decorated with ribands and paper (in which, if they can get one, is a little bird, to represent the wren), and repeat the following verse, or something of the same kind:

> *The wren, the wren, the king of all birds,*
> *Was caught on St. Stephen's day in the firs,*
> *Although he is little, his honour is great;*
> *So rise up, kind madame, and give us a treat.*
> *Up with the kettle, and down with the pan;*
> *A penny, or twopence, to bury the wren.* *
> *Your pocket full of money, and your cellar full of beer,*
> *I wish you all a merry Christmas, and a happy new year.*

*Pronounced here always as wran.

This ancient custom is, of course, derived from home, as well as that of the mummers, who assemble on New Year's day; the former from Ireland probably, the latter from the West of England.

There was, and still is, a sort of saturnalia amongst the lower classes, in St. John's particularly, and which lasts three days, commencing at Christmas, with boys only.

The mummers prepare, before the New Year, dresses of all possible shapes and hues, most of which are something like those of harlequin and the clown in pantomimes, but the general colour is white, with sundry bedaubments of tinsel and paint. A huge paper cocked hat is one favourite headpiece, and every one, among the gentlemen, excepting the captain or leader, and his two or three assistants, is masked. The ladies are represented by young fishermen, who are painted, but not masked. Some of the masks are very grotesque, and the fools or clowns are furnished with thongs and bladders, with which they belabour the exterior mob. Much ingenuity is observable in the style of the cocked hats, which are surmounted with all sorts of things, feathers in profusion, paper models of ships, etc.

They go to Government House first, and then round to the inhabitants; and it has been customary to make the captain a present of money for a ball, which is given at the end of the carnival, if it may be so styled.

They perform, at those houses which admit them, a sort of play, in which the unmasked characters only take part, and which is very long and tiresome after once hearing. It is a dialogue between the captain and a sailor, and commences with Alexander the Great, and continues down to Nelson and Wellington. They are both armed with swords, and a mock fight goes on all the while, till one is supposed to be slain, when the doctor is called in to bring him to life again. ❄

from *Newfoundland in 1842*

In 1842, British huntsman and sealer Sir Richard Bonnycastle visited Newfoundland. He chronicled his North American adventures and observations on local customs in two large volumes.

Dogs' Dinner BY TONY ONRAET

*T*he last Christmas I spent with my dogs was in 1938. I did not think of it at the time as anything except just one Christmas in a merry sequence we had spent together, but war broke out eight months later, and I left them to join up. A grand occasion we made of it. I had brought a good catch of fish home from the trapline two days earlier, also three lynx—big bobtails, catlike, with beautiful pelts and meat as white and tender as spring chicken. I kept one of the lynx for myself and cooked two for the dogs, along with half a dozen rabbits and half a dozen ptarmigan.

When I went to dig up my big ten-gallon cooking-pot from under the snow, those dogs knew it was feasting time. They howled, in chorus. "Christmas, boys!" I told them. They howled the harder.

It was a typical Christmas for those parts. The Northern Lights were dancing. They shoot right across the sky with terrifying rapidity, and all the colours of the rainbow are there: green and purple, red and yellow dominant.

Many pictures come and go as I look back. Maybe I am standing at the cabin door, smoking a good tobacco, content in the knowledge that there's a well-fed team of huskies near by. Maybe I am sitting inside the cabin, reading a good book in front of a hearty, flame-topped Christmas fire with plenty of dry wood to replenish it when necessary; a sizeable number of pelts hanging on the walls, and that bottle of rum I brought with me for medicinal purposes—in September; and again I am conscious of those happy dogs outside. But whatever it is, I have kept the memory keen and shall always do so, especially as I am sadly aware that I cannot ever again spend Christmas with those same dogs. ❄

from *Sixty Below*

French-Canadian outdoorsman Tony Onraet spent many years in the North, around Great Bear Lake, hunting and trapping.

Trout Lake Christmas BY HENRY BEER

KASLO, BRITISH COLUMBIA JANUARY 6, 1905

Dear Editor,

The following brief account of how the Archdeacon of Kootenay spent his last Christmas Day may be interesting to the readers of *Far West*.

On Friday, December 23rd, he left home at 11 o'clock, and went by steamboat to Lardo, twenty miles, then took a train for thirty-four miles, and was then carried by another small steamer another sixteen miles to Trout Lake Village. Thus he went seventy miles in all to hold his Christmas Service.

It was dark when he landed, and he went direct to the vacant Vicarage, for there is no resident clergyman at present. There was nearly two feet of snow on the ground, and the Vicarage was cold and dark. However, the Archdeacon found a lamp in the house, and there was an axe and wood in an outer shed, so he soon split some wood and made himself a fire. Some of the good people had placed in the Vicarage some bread, butter, tea, sugar, and a few other things, and a pail of water. So the Archdeacon was soon comfortably seated at a supper cooked by himself. One of the ladies of the parish had already made the bed, so after an hour or so of reading, and without seeing a single member of the congregation, the Archdeacon turned in, and had a good night's sleep.

Before daylight the next morning he was up and busy. He lit his fire, got his breakfast of porridge and toast, swept his house, made his bed, washed his dishes, split a large supply of wood to do over Christmas Day. Meantime he kept a large dish of snow on the stove and soon had a good pail of water.

Then he prepared the Church for the next day's Service. He swept the Church out, laid in a good supply of wood, shovelled the snow from the steps of the Church, and made paths for the congregation.

All this kept him busy as a nailer until it was time to cook his mid-day meal, which consisted of two kippered herrings, bread and the inevitable tea. The afternoon was spent in visiting the parishioners, and he was invited to five o'clock dinner. He retired to rest at 10 at night, pretty well tired out.

Christmas morning he was up before daylight again, made his breakfast and bed, cleaned up the house, lit the Church fires, and made ready for the Service of the day.

A congregation of sixteen persons assembled at 11, and six remained for Holy Communion. In the afternoon, the Archdeacon told the Sunday School children the story of the birth of Christ, to which they listened with the most interested attention. In the evening, the congregation was about as large as in the morning. Christmas dinner was partaken of with one of the Church families.

In the two Services we sang the good old hymns, but there was not a sprig of Christmas decorations or a carol, and, altogether, I suspect it was a violent contrast to the Services enjoyed by those who will read this account of Christmas Day in Trout Lake, British Columbia.

I can fancy some of our Church dignitaries in England having to sweep and cook, and light church fires, and shovel snow, and do all kinds of janitor's work.

On Monday the Archdeacon returned over the seventy-odd miles to his home, having spent four days of hard work to hold service with this small congregation, and having spent the first Christmas in forty years away from home.

It may be some of my readers may learn from this brief account how entirely different is a clergyman's life in the frontiers of Colonies to that of a clergyman in England, and how entirely out of place would a namby-pamby clergyman be in such circumstances. A man must be able to look after himself out here, as well be a faithful, diligent clergyman.

H. Beer, Archdeacon ❄

from *Work for the Far West—Anglican Archives 1904–1907*

The Stove BY ADJUTOR RIVARD

QUEBEC 1920S

*T*hrough months of cold, now loud, now low, it murmers an unfailing
tune; in those still nights which summon the spirits out to dance
across the serene northern sky, the stove's voice is even and regular and
reassuring; but when the north-east'er rages, shrieking as it battles with
the leafless trees, the stove roars angry defiance. It shields the swelling
from the fierce cold, and the comforting warmth rises to the dark rafters
and spreads to every corner of the house, even to the best room which no
one enters except on days of feasting or mourning. It thaws the powdery
snow sifting unkindly beneath the door that cannot shut it out, toasts little
red toes, warms the good soup to steaming.

The very soul of the house is it. Should the fire die within, and the
plume of smoke vanish from the chimney, and the purr of its draught suddenly fall silent, the house would swiftly be lifeless. "Dead hearths, dead
households." And the Canadian stove is as trusty a custodian of old tradition
as ever was the hearth.

At dusk the neighbours drop in for a pipe; they arrive plastered with
snow, and the stove is welcome to their hands stiffened with the cold.
When they are grouped about its door, and the light has circled till all the
pipes are going, this stove of the habitant likes to be entertained with talk
of the land hard-gripped by the autumn frosts, of outbuildings in course
of repair, of routine work on the farm and the monotonous labours of
winters, of beasts cared for, wheat in barn, the sugar-bush that is to be
tapped, the chances of the future crop. On Christmas Eve it was almost as
bright as day in the hay-mow, and that means a light stand of wheat next

summer . . . Last year the presage was the other way about, and, sure enough, we had a heavy yield to the very fences . . . In the spring we shall hire Pierre, the son of Gregoire; he ploughs a sight better than the rest of them and takes more sod . . . This evening's snowfall has nearly hidden the little trees marking the winter road; we shall have to be up tomorrow with the first streak of dawn to break a way through before the roadmaster comes along, for if he takes a fancy to go by early there will surely be a fine to pay . . . He is not over-considerate, is the roadmaster; he puts you to no end of trouble for a trifle of a drift; and there are pitch-holes opposite his own place, too. ❄

from *Chez Nous (Our Old Quebec Home)*, translated by W.H. Blake—an account of life in rural Quebec and essays about the implements used in the home and on the farm

Wishing Happiness BY HENRY VAN DYKE

SOUTHERN NEW BRUNSWICK 1905

Dirk Tempelman-Kluit photo

*T*he finest Christmas gift is not the one that costs the most money, but the one that carries the most love.

But how seldom Christmas comes—only once a year; and how soon it is over—a night and a day! If that is the whole of it, it seems not much more durable than the little toys that one buys of a fakir on the street-corner. They run for an hour, and then the spring breaks, and the legs come off, and nothing remains but a contribution to the dust.

But surely that need not and ought not to be the whole of Christmas—only a single day of generosity, ransomed from the dull servitude of a selfish year—only a single night of merry-making, celebrated in the slave-quarters of a selfish race! If every gift is the token of a personal thought, a friendly feeling, an unselfish interest in the joy of others, then the thought, the feeling, the interest, may remain after the gift is made.

The little present, or the rare and long-wished-for gift (it matters not whether the vessel be of gold, or silver, or iron, or wood, or clay, or just a small bit of birchbark folded into a cup) may carry a message something like this:

I am thinking of you today, because it is Christmas, and I wish you happiness, and tomorrow, because it will be the day after Christmas, I shall still wish you happiness; and so on, clear through the year. I may not be able to tell you about it every day, because I may be far away; or because both of us may be very busy; or perhaps because I cannot afford to pay the postage on so many letters or find the time to write them.

But that makes no difference. The thought and wish will be here just the same. In my work and the business of life, I mean to try not to be unfair to you or injure you in any way. In my pleasure, if we can be together, I would like to share the fun with you. Whatever joy or success comes to you will make me glad. Without pretense, and in plain words, good will to you is what I mean, in the spirit of Christmas.

After all, Christmas-living is the best kind of Christmas-giving. ❄

from *A Very Victorian Christmas*—a booklet of Christmas poems, stories and thoughts, mostly about New Brunswick

Sugared Igloos BY IAN AND SALLY WILSON

*A*s Sally and I wandered back home in the fading light of early afternoon, we saw a group of twenty or thirty children gathered outside the community hall. I was just about to ask what the occasion was, when a colourfully dressed man came sliding through town on a qamutik [long sled] pulled by four huskies. As he passed the group of eager children, he tossed handfuls of candies to them.

This was Baker Lake's version of Christmas. It was quviasukvik, a time to be happy. During the darkest and coldest days of winter, endless festivities were planned to brighten the spirits of everyone in the village. We looked forward to a few days off, time away from building igloos and preparing for our winter trip.

Christmas was pleasantly different from the lights and glitter of the south. Duffel socks were used for stockings, and caribou antlers draped in tinsel were fitting decorations for an Arctic Christmas. With the nearest forest hundreds of kilometres away, there were no real Christmas trees and few artificial ones.

For Christmas dinner, Mamaaq laid out a selection of the best chunks of caribou and trout. Tea and bannock completed the meal. Chuba made his specialty for dessert: bannock cooked in rings like large doughnuts and sprinkled with sugar. Our contribution to the festivities was to make sugar cookies.

"What shape would you like to make your cookies?" Sally asked Christina. We had already fashioned cutouts for Carolina in the shape of an igloo and a qamutik.

"An ulu [scraping knife]. And a tree—the kind you have in the south. I have some green sparkles I could put on it."

As we munched on sugar-sprinkled igloos and qamutiks, we joined the family to open presents. Sally and I opened gifts that our friends had made, all for our upcoming trip across the land. Singaqti had made us an ajagaak, a bone game for the long nights he knew we would be spending in igloos. Sally received a hand-knitted toque with her name in Inuktitut from Amma's daughter. Another friend has braided a colourful tapsi [a parka sash] for me to tie around my atigi [caribou-skin inner parka].

"Look at this!" Sally said to me as she unwrapped a present from Mamaaq.

"What is it?" The piece of carved wood looked much like a paddle used in old British private schools for discipline.

"It's a snow-beater," Sally explained. "We have to beat the snow off our caribou-skin clothes at the end of each day." These thoughtful gifts would always be a reminder of the special friends we had met in Baker Lake.

The household was bustling with activity until two in the morning. Matthew pushed a toy snowmobile up and down the hallway, and the girls played with identical dolls.

"There was only one kind of doll at the store," Peter told me later. We discovered that the lack of selection in the store had some amusing side effects—many young girls received identical dolls, and most young boys had identical toy snowmobiles. Green sleds, bright orange toques, and pink mitts were also seen in great abundance.

For the following week, the community was busy with the many celebrations of quviasukvik. Each day, during the few hours of daylight, we watched dog-team races, snowmobile races and other outdoor contests. ❄

from *Arctic Adventures: Exploring Canada's North by Canoe and Dog Team*

In 12 months, Ian and Sally Wilson travelled more than 3,500 kilometres by canoe and dog team across Canada's Arctic.

SHANTY AT EAGLE'S NEST.

A Wondrous Snowshoe Trail

BY ROBERT RENISON

ALBANY, ONTARIO 1898

*T*he Christmas season at Albany was an inspiring time. The Hudson's Bay Company Post was like a feudal castle dominating the scene in the little village near the mouth of one of the greatest rivers in Ontario. It was the hunting season and most of the Indian families were away. Two days before Christmas I stood on the bank of the river. Among the willows along the shore a mile away I saw what looked like a black serpent winding its way down the slope. It was a Cree family on the march.

The father walked ahead on snowshoes, breaking the trail. He was followed by his wife with a papoose wrapped in a rabbit-skin blanket on her back. Four half-starved dogs hauled a toboggan on which the family's belongings were packed, and three half-grown children brought up the rear. They had travelled for five days and slept out under the north wind for five nights. One thing brought them: like the Magi of old, they came to see a sign.

By Christmas eve there were a hundred wigwams around the church, the interior of which had been transformed. A small cedar tree had been nailed to the end of each pew; a silver star made from a new tin plate had been hung on wire from the ceiling and incredible flowers had been fashioned by deft hands from coloured paper. The floor had been scrubbed and the box stove shone like black marble.

On Christmas morning, while it was still dark, the church was filled; the men on one side and the women on the other. So rigid is this rule that no boy older than five or six sits on his mother's side of the church. Every man wore new embroidered moccasins and every woman a new tartan shawl. They sang in their own tongue, in their soft voices, the songs that had been sung in Europe since the Middle Ages. Their moccasined feet moved silently as bronze-faced hunters and their sons made their Communion, while wives, waiting their turns, bared their breasts to nurse their babies at the first whimper.

It was a moving experience to watch their faces as they listened to the wonderous Christmas story. To them the manger was lined with spruce boughs, as were their wigwams. They had never seen sheep, so they pictured the deer of the forest peering through the trees. And it was a snow-shoe trail they saw stretching far to the East whence the Medicine Men came.

It is heartening to remember that it was not in Jerusalem or in Rome that the Christmas message was heard. It was under the stars that the first Christmas congregation gathered. The stained-glass windows were in the sky, the congregation who heard the choir were alone with their flocks.

The next day the children had their hour. A Christmas tree stood in the schoolhouse, lighted with three-inch wax candles wedged in a hundred empty rifle cartridge cases which had been tied to the branches. Bags of candies, shining like rubies, topaz, and emeralds waited for every child. A blue goose, frozen in its feathers, hung high on the tree for the oldest grandmother.

The octave ended on New Year's day, when the ancient Scottish tradition of the state festival was observed at every Hudson's Bay Company Post. It was the custom for every Indian to call at the Factory—the house of the Company Manager—and at the mission house.

That night the Northern Lights came out to serenade the stars.

Dear God, they shone in Palestine
Like this, and yon pale moon serene
Looked down among the lowly kine;
On Mary and the Nazarene.

The Angels called from deep to deep.
The burning heavens felt the thrill,
Startling the flocks of silly sheep
And lonely shepherds on the hill.

Next morning the wigwams were down. The Indians had gone. They departed unto their own home another way. ❄

from *One Day at a Time: The Autobiography of Robert John Renison*

Dedicated missionary Robert Renison never forgot his first love of the northern missions where he gained experience. He inspired many Native people to become priests.

Christmas BY ALBERT DURRANT WATSON

ONTARIO 1924

Give each new day its
Own good cheer
All other days apart,
And every day
Throughout the year
Keep Christmas in your heart.

from *The Poetical Works of Albert Durrant Watson*

The now near-forgotten Dr. Watson (1859–1926), Ontario-born grandson of a Wellington cavalryman at Waterloo, was ranked in 1908 by Toronto's *Sunday World* arts critic as "at once among the greater poets of Canada."

Permissions

Every effort has been made to trace the ownership of copyright material in this text. The editor and the publisher welcome any information enabling them to rectify any reference or credit in subsequent editions.

"The First Canadian Christmas Carol" courtesy of Mission Press, from *Brébeuf in Song and Verse*, 1975. Page 19.

"Log Cabin Christmas" courtesy of Mrs. Joan Renison, from *One Day at a Time: The Autobiography of Robert John Renison* by Robert Renison, 1957. Page 23.

"North Pole Athletic Club" courtesy of Mrs. Brenda Rasky, from *Explorers of the North: The North Pole or Bust* by Frank Rasky, 1977. Page 26.

"Upon a Midnight Clear" from *Heart of a Stranger* by Margaret Laurence. By permission of McClelland & Stewart Ltd. Page 29.

"Construction Camp Christmas" courtesy of Caitlin Press, from *The Far Land* by Eva MacLean, 1993. Page 35.

"Reveillon" courtesy of Shoreline Books, from *Walk Alone Together: Portrait of a French-English Marriage* by A. Margaret Caza, 1990. Page 39.

Latulippe Family Tourtières recipe courtesy of Claudette Sakamoto, 2005. Page 43.

"Unfortunate Santa Claus" courtesy of the *Saint John Telegraph-Journal*, 1892. Page 44.

"Lost Moose" courtesy of publisher Sara Harder, Sardis, BC, from *The Homemade Brass Plate: The Story of a Pioneer Doctor in Northern Alberta* by Dr. Mary Percy Jackson, 1988. Page 49.

"A Railroad Christmas" courtesy of Fifth House Publishers, from *Sunny Side Up: Fond Memories of Prairie Life in the 1930s* by Eileen Comstock, 2001. Page 51.

"Anne and More" from *The Green Gables Letters from L.M. Montgomery to Ephraim Weber, 1905–1909*, edited by Wilfrid Eggleston (Borealis Press, Ottawa: 1981) and reprinted with the permission of Ruth Macdonald. *L.M. Montgomery* is a trademark of L.M. Montgomery Inc. and its owners. Page 53.

"Celebrations at the Jardin de l'enfance" courtesy of Vehicule Press, from *Memoirs of a Less Travelled Road: A Historian's Life* by Marcel Trudel, 1987. Page 57.

"How Santa Claus Came to Cape St. Anthony" courtesy of the International Grenfell Mission. Page 61.

"Christmas at the Sour Dough Hotel" courtesy of Caitlin Press, from *Spirit of the Yukon* by June Cruickshank Lunny, 1992. Page 69.

"The Freeport Angel" courtesy of Rita Moir, from *Survival Gear*, 1994. Page 71.

"Christmas Parade" courtesy of Marsha Boulton, from *Letters from the Country: Omnibus*, 2001. Page 75.

"The Trapper's Christmas Eve" courtesy of the estate of Robert Service, from *Collected Poems of Robert Service*, Dodd, Mead & Co. 1961. Page 79.

"The Front-room" courtesy of Broadview Press, from *Nellie McClung: The Complete Autobiography: Clearing in the West & The Stream Runs Fast*, a 2003 re-issue in one volume with new introduction and notes by Veronica Jane Strong-Boag and Michelle Lynn Rosa, 1935. Page 83.

286

"The Indians' Christmas Tree" courtesy of the Archives of the Anglican Provincial Synod of British Columbia and Yukon, from the *Diocese of New Westminster, Vol. 1, 1889–1896.* Page 87.

"The Teddy Bear Coat" courtesy of *Voice for Island Seniors*, Prince Edward Island, 2003: www.gov.pe.ca/christmas/seniors. Page 93.

"Moving Day" courtesy of the City of Burnaby, from *Pioneer Tales of Burnaby*, edited by Michael Sone, 1987. Page 95.

"The Toy Shop" courtesy of Fifth House Publishers, from *Days Gone By: Jack Peach on Calgary's Past* by Jack Peach, 1993. Page 107.

"Next Year Country" courtesy of Judy Schultz, from *Mamie's Children: Three Generations of Prairie Women*, 1997. Page 123.

"A Barrens Christmas" courtesy of Edward Nuffield, from *Samual Hearne: Journey to the Coppermine River, 1769–1772*, 2001. Page 127.

"Man's Best Friend" courtesy of Audrey Smedley-L'Heureux, from *From Trail to Rail— Settlement Begins 1905–1914, The Story as Told by People Who Were There*, 1990. Page 129.

"The First Christmas Tree" courtesy of Mrs. Justine Housser. Page 131.

"A Christmas Kiss" courtesy of Gwyneth J. Whilsmith, from *Hear the Pennies Dropping*, 1987. Page 133.

"A True Believer" courtesy of Broadview Press, from *Nellie McClung: The Complete Autobiography: A Clearing in the West & The Stream Runs Fast*, edited by Veronica Jane Strong-Boag and Michelle Lynn Rosa, 1935. Page 137.

"Christmas Orange" courtesy of David Weale, from *Them Times*, 1992. Page 139.

"Old Chum and Scrooge" courtesy of Shoreline Books, from *Girl in a Red River Coat* by Mary Peate, 2000. Page 143.

"Special Parcel" courtesy of Rita Joe, from *The Song of Rita Joe*, 1996. Page 153.

"Christmas Diet" courtesy of the Historical Society of Alberta, from *Challenge of the Homestead: Peace River Letters of Clyde and Myrle Campbell 1919–1924* by Clyde and Myrle Campbell, 1988. Page 159.

"Lost in the Mountains on Christmas Day" courtesy of Heritage House Publishers, from *Tales of a Pioneer Journalist* by David William Higgins, 1996. Page 161.

"Our Radio City Music Hall" courtesy of Marjorie Barr Pratt, from *Recollections of a Homesteader's Daughter*, 1997. Page 171.

Carrot Pudding recipe courtesy of Christine Dow, 2005. Page 181.

"Doll's Delight" courtesy of Shoreline Press, from *Looking Back* by Bess Burrows Rivett, 1996. Page 185.

"Merry-Go-Round" courtesy of Saunders of Toronto, a Division of Thomas Allan & Son, Ltd., from *The Galloping Gospel* by Angus H. MacLean, 1966. Page 191.

"Our Field of Trees" courtesy of Betty Kirchhofer, from the *Saskatchewan Senior*, 2003. Page 195.

"Wedding Journey" courtesy of University of Toronto Press, from *Young Mr. Smith in Upper Canada* edited and annotated by Mary Larratt Smith, 1980. Page 201.

"Christmas in the Klondike" by Rev. A.E. Hetherington, from the *Methodist Recorder*, 1906, courtesy of United Church B.C. Conference Archives. Page 203.

"Red and White" courtesy of Fred Edge, from *The Iron Rose: The Life of Charlotte Ross, MD*, 1992. Page 209.

"Kamloops Conversion" courtesy of the Archives of the Anglican Provincial Synod of British Columbia and Yukon, from the *Churchman's Gazette*, 1888. Page 214.

"The Doll" by Syd Clay, courtesy of *Voice for Island Seniors*, 1996. Page 217.

"Rocket Racer Sled" courtesy of Gus Barrett, from the *Moccasin Telegraph*, 2004. Page 221.

"A Love Story" courtesy of Broadview Press, from *A Love Story from Nineteenth Century Quebec: The Diary of George Stephen Jones* by George Stephen Jones, 1989. Page 229.

"Wily Fox" excerpt from *Forty Years for Labrador* by Sir Wilfred Grenfell. Copyright renewed 1960 by Rosamond Grenfell Shaw. Reprinted by permission of Houghton Mifflin Company. Page 245.

"Paper Planes" courtesy of Shoreline Press, from *Girl in a Sloppy Joe Sweater: Life on the Canadian Home Front During World War II* by Mary Peate, 2002. Page 247.

"Candles for Christmas" courtesy of Alberta Folklore and Local History Collection, University of Alberta Libraries, 2004. Page 251.

"The Surprise" courtesy of Ada L. Sudsbury, 2005. Page 253.

"Gourmet Christmas" courtesy of Whitecap Books Ltd., from *A Year in Niagara: The People and Food of Wine Country* by Kathleen Sloan-McIntosh, 2002. Page 257.

"St. Mary's Hospital Christmas Bazaar" courtesy of Whitecap Books Ltd., from *Women of the Klondike* by Frances Backhouse, 2002. Page 260.

"Trout Lake Christmas" by Henry Beer courtesy of Archives of the Anglican Provincial Synod of British Columbia and Yukon, from *Work for the Far West*, 1904–1907. Page 267.

"Wishing Happiness" by Henry Van Dyke courtesy of David Goss, from *A Very Victorian Christmas*, 2003. Page 273.

"Sugared Igloos" courtesy of Gordon Soules Book Publishers Ltd., from *Arctic Adventures: Exploring Canada's North by Canoe and Dog Team* by Ian and Sally Wilson, 1992. Page 275.

"A Wondrous Snowshoe Trail" courtesy of Mrs. Joan Renison, from *One Day at a Time: The Autobiography of Robert John Renison* by Robert Renison, 1957. Page 279.

Archer, S.A.: Charlotte Selina: *A Heroine of the North: Memoirs of Charlotte Selina Bompas.* MacMillan Company of Canada, Ltd. pp. 103–104.

Ballantyne, Robert M.: *Hudson's Bay: or Every-day Life in the Wilds of North America During Six Years' Residence in the Territories of the Honourable Hudson's Bay Company.* Thomas Nelson and Sons. pp. 99–105.

Bonnycastle, Sir Richard Henry: *Newfoundland in 1842, a Sequel to The Canadas in 1841* (Vol.1). Henry Colburn, 1842. pp. 138–140.

Bullock-Webster, Harry: *Memories of Sport and Travel Fifty Years Ago: From the Hudson's Bay Company to New Zealand.* Whitcombe and Tombs Ltd., 1938. pp. 67–68.

Carr, Emily: *The Book of Small.* Clarke, Irwin, 1942. pp. 171–175, edited by Charles Wendell Townsend.

Captain Cartwright and His Labrador Journal, edited by Margaret Howard Blom and Thomas E. Blom. Dana Estes & Co., 1911. pp. 57–58 and 96–97.

de Boilieu, Lambert: *Recollections of Labrador Life.* Ryerson Press, 1969. pp. 48–51.

Ewing, Juliana H.: *Canada Home: Juliana Horatia Ewing's Fredericton Letters, 1867–1869.* UBC Press, 1983. pp. 86–87.

Fairfax, Dick: *So Soon Forgotten.* Western Producer Prairie Books, 1955. pp. 38–39.

Fraser, Sarah: *Pasture Spruce: A Story of Rural Life in Nova Scotia at the Turn of the Century.* Petheric Press, 1971. pp. 126–127.

Gibson, Morris: *A Doctor in the West.* Collins, 1988. pp. 127–130.

Grey Owl: *Pilgrims of the Wild*. MacMillan Company of Canada, Ltd., 1939. pp. 143–147.

Ham, George H.: *Reminiscences of a Raconteur Between the '40s and '20s*. The Musson Book Company Ltd., 1921. pp. 220–221.

Head, George: *Forest Scenes and Incidents in the Wilds of North America*. J. Murray, 1829.

Hunter, Anne: *The Journal of General Sir Martin Hunter and Some Letters of His Wife, Lady Hunter*. Edinburgh Press, 1894.

Johnston, Sheila M.F.: *Buckskin and Broadcloth: A Celebration of E. Pauline Johnson— Tekahionwake, 1861–1913*. Natural Heritage Books, 1997. pp. 60, 86–88.

Leacock, Stephen: *Christmas with Stephen Leacock*. National Heritage Books, 1988. pp. 76–79.

McTavish, George S.: *Behind the Palisades: An Autobiography*. Gray's Publishing Ltd., 1963. pp. 66–70.

Moodie, Susanna: *Roughing It in the Bush, or Forest Life in Canada*. Coles Publishing Company, 1974. pp. 175–176.

Muir, Earl St. C.: *Poems of the Prairie*. The Vancouver Poetry Society, 1930. p. 11.

Onraet, Tony: *Sixty Below*. Jonathan Cape, Toronto: 1944. pp. 125–126.

Pethick, Derek: *Vancouver: The Pioneer Years 1774–1886*. Sunfire Publishers, 1984. p. 178.

Pringle, George C.F.: *Adventures in Service*. McClelland & Stewart Ltd. 1929. pp. 96–114 (edited).

Rivard, Adjutor: *Chez Nous (Our Old Quebec Home)*. McClelland & Stewart Ltd. 1924. pp. 50–51.

Thompson, Capt. George S.: *Up To Date, or The Life of a Lumberman*. 1895. p. 226.

Van Dyke, Henry: *A Very Victorian Christmas*. 2003.

Watson, Albert Durrant: *The Poetical Works of Albert Durrant Watson*. Ryerson Press, 1924. p. 115.

Yorke, W. Milton: *Tales of the Porcupine Trails*. The Musson Book Company, 1911. p. 94.